# ARKANSAS

## AN ILLUSTRATED ATLAS

*Tom Paradise*

**BUTLER CENTER BOOKS**

UNIVERSITY OF ARKANSAS

DIANE D. BLAIR CENTER
*of Southern Politics & Society*

This book was published in collaboration with the Diane D. Blair Center of Southern Politics & Society at the University of Arkansas in Fayetteville.

**www.butlercenter.org**

The Butler Center for Arkansas Studies
Central Arkansas Library System
100 Rock Street
Little Rock, AR 72201

Project Manager: Rod Lorenzen
Copyeditor: Ali Welky
Art Director: Mike Keckhaver
Contributors: Fiona Davidson PhD, Angie Maxwell PhD, Margaret Reid PhD, John Van Brahana PhD
Cartographers: Haunani Verzon (Map & Graphics Coordinator), Rashauna "Coco" Mickens, Michele L. McKee

Library of Congress Cataloging-in-Publication Data

Paradise, Thomas R.
  Arkansas: an illustrated atlas / by Tom Paradise
  1 atlas (56 p.) : ill., col. maps; 28 cm.
  ISBN-13: 978-1-935106-49-4 (alk. paper)
  ISBN-10: 1-935106-35-X
  1. Arkansas--Maps. 2. Arkansas--History. 3. Atlases. I. Title. II. Title: Arkansas, an Illustrated Atlas.
  G1355.P2 2010
  912.767--dc22
                              2010075007

This book is printed on archival-quality paper that meets requirements of the American National Standard for Information Sciences, Permanence of Paper, Printed Library Materials, ANSI Z39.48-1984.

*An Illustrated Atlas of ARKANSAS*

# Table of Contents

| | |
|---|---|
| 4-5 | Where on Earth Are We? |
| 6-7 | Round Planet to Flat Map |
| 8-9 | Cartography, Maps, and Scale |
| 10-11 | Maps and Interpretation |
| 12-13 | Elevation and Relief |
| 14-15 | Five Themes of Geography |
| 16-17 | Prehistory in Arkansas |
| 18-19 | History in Arkansas |
| 20-21 | Population and Demography |
| 22-23 | Industry and Economy |
| 24-25 | Politics in Arkansas |
| 26-27 | Weather and Water |
| 28-29 | Agriculture in Arkansas |
| 30-31 | Caves and Karst |
| 32-33 | Geology of Arkansas |
| 34-35 | Diamonds in Arkansas |
| 36-37 | Ecosystems of Arkansas |
| 38-39 | Endangered Species and Protected Lands |
| 40-41 | Parks and Sites in Arkansas |
| 42-43 | Lakes and Dams |
| 44-45 | Hunting in Arkansas |
| 46-47 | Fishing in Arkansas |
| 48-49 | Hazards and Disasters |
| 50-51 | Glossary |
| 52 | Unique Arkansas! |
| 53 | Gazetteer |
| 54-55 | Reference Maps of Arkansas |
| 56 | How to Learn More |

Although it is unique and diverse, Arkansas represents a medium-sized state in the United States, and sits on a relatively small planet in our solar system. Arkansas represents 1.4% of the total area of the country and when we compare the largest planet, Jupiter, to Earth, Jupiter is 1,382 times bigger in volume! When we compare Arkansas to Earth, the land area of Earth is 1,746 times larger than Arkansas (92,547,000 square miles vs. 53,179 square miles) and 5,980 times larger when comparing Earth's total surface area to Arkansas.

*In 2010, there were more than 550 satellites orbiting Earth, taking pictures and collecting data.*

*We live on the third planet from the Sun, which is the fifth largest of eight planets in our solar system. Earth is the only one covered with a blanket of liquid water, so it is sometimes called the Blue Planet, Terra, or even the "Big Blue Marble."*

*Scientists estimate Earth's age at 4.54 billion years, with life appearing in its first billion years. About 70% of the surface is covered with water: 97% saltwater and 3% fresh. Earth is the only place in the solar system where life is known to exist (for now). Earth is home to millions of species, including humans, considered as the planet's dominant species. Human inhabitants can be grouped into differing categories, which can include about 200 independent sovereign states, which interact through commerce and trade, travel, war, and diplomacy.*

Arkansas

*This is a satellite photograph of Earth taken in 1992. Arkansas is highlighted in red. Notice the large white spiral of clouds and rain in the Gulf of Mexico – that's Hurricane Andrew.*

**Arkansas represents one of the most diverse states in the U.S., with a geography unlike any other place. The state's physical setting takes us from the deep valley and steep peaks of the Ozark and Ouachita mountains, to the broad plains and swamps of the Mississippi Delta. The economy is driven by retail, trucking, and poultry giants in addition to extensive petroleum, gas, and mineral resources. The cultural environment includes Native American, European, Asian, Latino, Pacific-Island, and African-American customs, rituals, traditions, and food. All of this variety and assortment is found across a spectacular landscape of feathery waterfalls, lush pastures, legendary caves, healing hot springs, extensive shopping and dining, and verdant vineyards, as well as fine arts, music, crafts, and a diamond mine! It is this uniqueness that brings great pride to all Arkansans.**

Greetings from ARKANSAS

**In this illustrated atlas of Arkansas, we will examine the geography of our state through its diverse landscapes, showing our many faces, aspects, settings, and people.**

**WELCOME to the NATURAL STATE!**

# Are We?

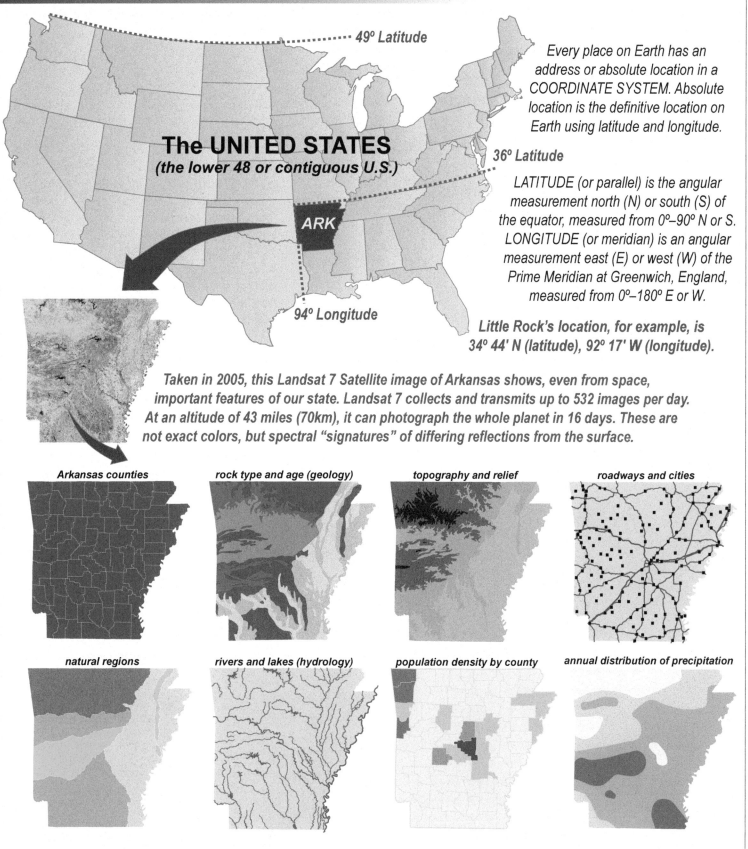

**The UNITED STATES**
*(the lower 48 or contiguous U.S.)*

49° Latitude

36° Latitude

94° Longitude

ARK

Every place on Earth has an address or absolute location in a COORDINATE SYSTEM. Absolute location is the definitive location on Earth using latitude and longitude.

LATITUDE (or parallel) is the angular measurement north (N) or south (S) of the equator, measured from 0°–90° N or S. LONGITUDE (or meridian) is an angular measurement east (E) or west (W) of the Prime Meridian at Greenwich, England, measured from 0°–180° E or W.

*Little Rock's location, for example, is 34° 44' N (latitude), 92° 17' W (longitude).*

Taken in 2005, this Landsat 7 Satellite image of Arkansas shows, even from space, important features of our state. Landsat 7 collects and transmits up to 532 images per day. At an altitude of 43 miles (70km), it can photograph the whole planet in 16 days. These are not exact colors, but spectral "signatures" of differing reflections from the surface.

**Arkansas counties**

**rock type and age (geology)**

**topography and relief**

**roadways and cities**

**natural regions**

**rivers and lakes (hydrology)**

**population density by county**

**annual distribution of precipitation**

*Arkansas is composed of diverse elements and features including political, cultural, physical, administrative, and economic characteristics. Geographers examine these features, their similarities, differences, and how they relate to other places. An atlas is a map collection of these features and relationships.*

**These are maps found throughout this atlas and are examples of various cartographic representations of the diverse aspects of Arkansas's milieu or the physical or social components of our landscape.**

We use maps to explain and represent our world and universe, and cartography is the field of studying and making maps. Map-making is a small part of the field since cartography also includes the study, psychology, use, technology, and history of mapping and map-makers. It is studied in geography programs in schools and universities around the world.

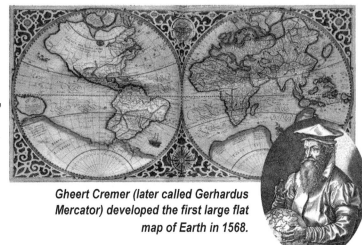

*Gheert Cremer (later called Gerhardus Mercator) developed the first large flat map of Earth in 1568.*

*Gerhardus Mercator 1512–1594*

*How do we make flat maps when our planet isn't flat? Since our planet is a sphere or spheroid, when you flatten that curved surface you create distortion or "stretching." Landmasses change size and shape on the map, which we call distortion. Distortion on a flat map is greatest when the mapped area is farthest from the round part being mapped. For example, on the Mercator map here, since the equator on Earth was closest to the equator on the map, the distortion is the least, and areas farthest are the most!*

The Mercator projection was used by sailors and navigators to sail the seas, and it would later help in the discovery of the New World. This was one of the great maps of the world for hundreds of years. In this projection, distortion increases as you move closer to the polar areas. This is why on the map below that Greenland appears to be larger than Africa. In reality, Greenland is 836,100 square miles in area, while the African continent is 11,668,600 square miles—Africa is actually fourteen times larger than Greenland!

## How do cartographers create flat maps of a round world?

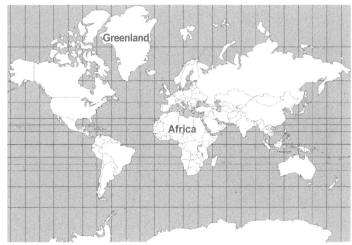

*When an orange is peeled, the peel can't be made flat without ripping. Projections are similar, since "ripping" or distortion occurs when cartographers make a flat map from a curved surface. So, nearly all flat maps are distorted (some a little, some a lot), since Earth is spherical and most maps are flat, except globes.*

# to Flat Map

Lines of longitude, or meridians, represent distances from east or west, as lines that join the North and South poles. These lines are all the same size and are spread apart the most at the equator. They narrow at the poles to overlap with each other. The planet rotates west to east, or counter-clockwise, when looking down on the North Pole. Establishing a starting longitude was more arbitrary than for latitude so a conference of different countries was held in 1883, creating 0° near London, England, in Greenwich (pronounced grehn-itch).

*The Greenwich Longitude is also called the Prime Meridian. Greenwich Mean Time is standardized to the Prime Meridian. Every 15° of longitude represents one hour of time passing on Earth. The Prime Meridian runs through western Europe and Africa while the 180° line runs from pole to pole on the other side of the planet through the Pacific Ocean—it is called the International Dateline. The Prime Meridian divides the planet into the Western and Eastern hemispheres.*

**An example of a Babylonian (600 BC) map on a clay tablet**

Prime Meridian (0° longitude)

Equator (0° latitude)

*This is the Armadillo Projection created by Erwin Raisz in 1943.*

*The Robinson Projection was created in 1963 by Arthur H. Robinson (1915–2004) and is one of the most widely used projections today. This projection is used to show the whole earth at once.*

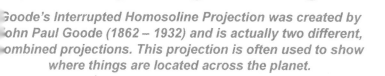

*Goode's Interrupted Homosoline Projection was created by John Paul Goode (1862 – 1932) and is actually two different, combined projections. This projection is often used to show where things are located across the planet.*

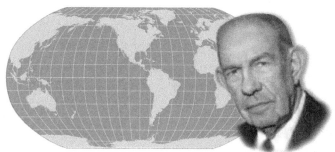

*Arthur H. Robinson*

A map is a visual representation of an area and its elements. It is a symbolic and thematic depiction of space showing the relationships between its spatial elements, such as objects, regions, and themes. Maps are usually two-dimensional (2-D), locationally accurate representations of three-dimensional (3-D) space. Nowadays we also create and use interactive 3-D maps. Although most maps have traditionally represented aspects of geography, maps may depict any space, at any scale, real or imagined. In addition to aspects of the landscape, such as buildings, roads, and mountains, cartographers can also map emotions, extraterrestrial objects, imagined places, or microscopic objects.

*What is the earliest known map is controversial. However, the earliest may be a wall painting from Turkey (then Asia Minor) from the city of Catal Huyuk. It has been dated to ca. 7000 BC. Other early maps include the 1600 BC wall painting in the Greek "House of the Admiral," and another from the Babylonian city Nippur dating from the 14th–12th centuries BC. The Greeks, Chinese, and Romans created a number of important early maps from 400 BC to AD 400. During this period the Chinese produced the first known celestial maps as well. However, it was Ptolemy's book* Geographia *in the 2nd century AD that contained his map of the known world.*

In the 8th–12th centuries, Arab geographers updated many of the earlier maps from Western Asia and the Mediterranean. During the Middle Ages, however, the field of cartography grew with the creation of the Mappa Mundi or "Maps of the World." More than one thousand Mappa Mundi have survived as maps and book illustrations. Renowned from this period is the Tabula Rogeriana, created in 1154 by Muhammad al-Idrisi for King Roger II of Sicily. The Tabula Rogeriana was the most accurate and widely used map of the known world until the 1500s.

*From the 15th to the 17th centuries, cartography developed quickly as a field and vocation. During the Age of Exploration, cartographers copied earlier maps or updated them based on new records and surveying innovations (some of which had been passed down for centuries) and drew their own based on explorers' observations, inventions (telescope), and new surveying techniques such as the magnetic compass (to the left) and the marine sextant (to the right). Since then, maps have been created in similar ways, only now we have computers to help us combine technologies to make better maps.*

# Maps, and Scale

Maps are representations of space, either on Earth or other celestial bodies. Without maps we cannot understand our places, spaces, locations, and surroundings. Maps enable our understanding of the world around us—local, regional, state, national, global, or universal. In the past they were always at a scale smaller than the actual space. Now, since we can map microscopic objects like bacteria or cells, these maps can represent something much larger than an actual space—a new direction in cartography!

*Scale is the relationship between the actual space to be mapped and the mapped area. It can be represented as a fraction (1/20,000), as a verbal scale (one inch represents one mile), or as a graphic scale in which a bar is used to illustrate a distance (see images below).*

*When a map represents a larger area like a continent, the scale will get smaller, since the fraction that represents the ratio of real space to map space gets smaller too.*

**Look at how the scale changes as the views of Lake Chicot change.**

*AR*

*100 miles*

*Arkansas*

*Memphis*

*Lake Chicot, Arkansas*

*Mississippi*

**In this satellite image, all of Arkansas is visible. The longest distance across Arkansas is from the northeast corner (near Piggott) to the southeast (near Ravana) at 325 miles. The graphic scale on the map shows 100 miles represented by one half inch. The representative fraction scale (or RF) is 1/12,500,000 or 1:12,500,000; one unit on the map (inch, foot, or meter) represents 12,500,000 similar units on Earth. This map is 12 million times smaller than the real Earth.**

*4 miles*

*Lake Chicot Village*

**Now we see a closeup of the southeast corner of the state at the border with the Mississippi River. The river is muddy and beige, while the lake is clear and dark blue-green. Now the scale represents only four miles for about one half inch. At this scale the representative fraction (RF) is 1/500,000 or 1:500,000.**

## DYK?

Since map scale is a ratio between map distance and real distance, it can be confusing. When the scale is large (and the fraction is large), then the map represents a small place like a backyard. This is weird because a "large scale" map can also refer to a big mapped area like North America (which is actually small scale)!

**Here we see a closeup of Lake Chicot. At this scale, houses and roads can be seen. This scale represents 800 feet on Earth for one half inch on the map. This represents an RF of 1/19,000 or 1:19,000. This is the largest scale on this page.**

*800 feet*

Cartographers illustrate objects and parts of the landscape in more simplistic ways, so that a map is easy and quick to use. A road may be portrayed as a line or a wide strip, while a structure might be a simple rectangle or a detailed building. Map scale determines how detailed the map can be. Large map scale (1:500, like a house) permits more detail, while small scale (1:500,000, like a country) allows only simple map representations.

When representing maps of urban or built-up areas, most maps show buildings and structures, roads and highways, parks, monuments, paths, and bodies of water (like ponds and rivers). More-detailed maps can differentiate between types of structures too, such as hospitals, schools, hotels, and government offices.

*This is a satellite photograph of our nation's capital, the District of Columbia (Washington DC). The city is located on the Potomac River between the states of Virginia and Maryland. The Washington DC metropolitan area has a population of 5.3 million, the ninth-largest metropolitan area in the country.*

**LEGEND**
- building
- park/lawn
- water
- footpath
- roadway

*This is a simple map of the photograph above of Washington DC. This is a thematic map since it illustrates the various elements of the landscape by using color to distinguish between them on the landscape: buildings and structures (red), grassy lawns and parks (green), non-motorized ways like pedestrian paths and bike trails (yellow), and roads for motorized transportation like cars, trucks, and buses (black).*

## *A good map is easy and fast to use!*

*A precise map and clear legend simplify the diverse and complicated aspects of the landscape into discrete elements. Look at this map with the legend and notice how much faster it is to interpret than the matching photograph above.*

# Interpretation

Here we see how aerial images can be represented as maps. Aerial maps are maps made from images taken from the air and can be very accurate since a photograph was used to create the map itself, using a technique called "digitizing." In digitizing, cartographers trace on top of a photograph to create the map.

*This photograph was taken from a satellite above the north part of Little Rock, Arkansas, along the banks of the Arkansas River. A photograph taken directly above Earth is called an orthophotograph.*

*The shadows cast from buildings can help geographers figure out the time of day, building height, and orientation of the photograph. Remote sensing uses photographs taken from planes or satellites, and photogrammetry uses measurements taken from aerial photographs to make maps that are used in aerial surveying.*

**Legends are map keys that explain the colors, shapes, or symbols used on the map to represent buildings, roads, and other features.**

*Maps take the essential elements on the landscape and filter out the less important things. Colors are used to help differentiate these elements but may not represent the actual color of the feature. On this map the built-up area (urban) is shown as yellow, while the structures are red. Cartographers use basemaps to accurately locate places, then add the thematic elements on top of the basemap to represent the essential aspects of the map (buildings, roads, land use, etc.).*

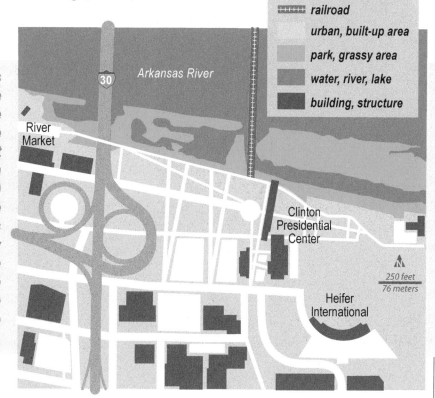

**LEGEND**

- interstate highway
- road, parking area
- railroad
- urban, built-up area
- park, grassy area
- water, river, lake
- building, structure

Arkansas River

30

River Market

Clinton Presidential Center

250 feet
76 meters

Heifer International

Elevation represents height above sea level, and topography is a description of a place that includes elevation and surface variations (both man-made and natural). Arkansas has a relief of 2,698 feet (822 meters), which is the difference between the highest point (2,753') and the lowest (55') in Arkansas. However, the relief of the U.S. is much more—14,787' for the continental U.S. and 20,620' (which is almost four miles) if we consider Alaska. Mount Denali in Alaska (formerly Mount McKinley) is the highest peak in the 50 states at 20,320'. Mount Whitney is the highest mountain in the lower 48 states at 14,505'. (Death Valley is the lowest point at -282'.) Interestingly, Mount Whitney and Death Valley are both in California and are only 88 miles apart!

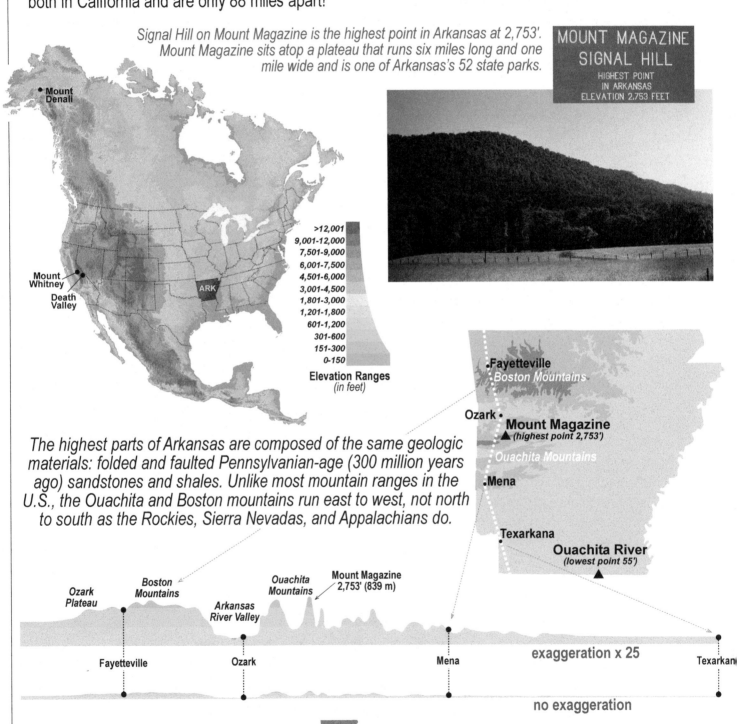

*Signal Hill on Mount Magazine is the highest point in Arkansas at 2,753'. Mount Magazine sits atop a plateau that runs six miles long and one mile wide and is one of Arkansas's 52 state parks.*

MOUNT MAGAZINE
SIGNAL HILL
HIGHEST POINT
IN ARKANSAS
ELEVATION 2,753 FEET

Mount Denali

Mount Whitney

Death Valley

ARK

>12,001
9,001-12,000
7,501-9,000
6,001-7,500
4,501-6,000
3,001-4,500
1,801-3,000
1,201-1,800
601-1,200
301-600
151-300
0-150

**Elevation Ranges**
*(in feet)*

Fayetteville
*Boston Mountains*

Ozark
**Mount Magazine**
▲ *(highest point 2,753')*

*Ouachita Mountains*

Mena

Texarkana
**Ouachita River**
*(lowest point 55')*
▲

*The highest parts of Arkansas are composed of the same geologic materials: folded and faulted Pennsylvanian-age (300 million years ago) sandstones and shales. Unlike most mountain ranges in the U.S., the Ouachita and Boston mountains run east to west, not north to south as the Rockies, Sierra Nevadas, and Appalachians do.*

Ozark Plateau

Boston Mountains

Arkansas River Valley

Ouachita Mountains

Mount Magazine 2,753' (839 m)

Fayetteville

Ozark

Mena

Texarkana

exaggeration x 25

no exaggeration

This topography or relief map shows the elevations across the state, above sea level.

Arkansas's topography is highest in the western and northern parts in the Ouachita and Boston mountains and Ozark Plateau. The lowest elevations lie in the eastern and southern parts of the state along the Mississippi River and its tributaries.

**2,401-3,000'**
**1,801-2,400'**
**1,201-1,800'**
**601-1,200'**
**301-600'**
**151-300'**
**0-150'**

*Ozark Plateau*

**Delta croplands**

*Ozark "holler" or foothill valley*

*Why is it usually warmer in the Arkansas River Valley than higher up in the Ozarks?*

Dry air rises in temperature 5.5°F for every 1,000 feet it descends (10°C/1,000m). Wet air, like in clouds, rain, or fog, rises in temperature 3.6°F for every 1,000 feet it drops (6.5°C/1,000m).

*Elevation has a big influence on temperature, shown in the environmental lapse rate (ELR). The ELR is how much the temperature decreases with elevation. Depending on whether the air is wet or dry, the temperature will drop with ascent or rise with descent.*

37.5°F
**Mt. Magazine**
*(2,753')*

45°F
**Paris**
*(400')*

45°F
**Havana**
*(400')*

*(IN WET AIR)*

North     South

*Saturated Air (wet adiabatic lapse rate)*

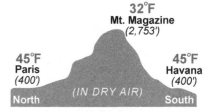

32°F
**Mt. Magazine**
*(2,753')*

45°F
**Paris**
*(400')*

45°F
**Havana**
*(400')*

*(IN DRY AIR)*

North     South

*Dry Air (dry adiabatic lapse rate)*

*For example, when it is 45°F in the Arkansas River Valley in Paris (400' elevation), it will be approximately 8°F cooler on Mount Magazine if it's rainy, or 13°F cooler and freezing on the mountain if it's clear.*

## What are the
# FIVE THEMES
## of Geography?

*Old Main, University of Arkansas, cultural feature*

The field of geography examines the location of our planet's features, processes, and changes. Some of these are natural features like the Arkansas River or the Ouachita Mountains, and some can be cultural or human-made elements of the landscape like buildings or farms. Geographers break down all of these elements into five themes—these are very important in our world since they can explain all that we see, use, make, or know.

*Geography is all around us.*

**Waterfall, Buffalo River Wilderness, natural feature**

# 2. LOCATION

*LOCATION is crucial because it explains where we can find things. Location can be described two ways: absolute and relative. Absolute location is a specific way of explaining where something is. We can use latitude and longitude for this. But when you tell your friend that your house is right across the street from your school, you are using relative location to explain where you live.*

*Riverwalk, Little Rock, Arkansas, cultural feature*

# 1. PLACE

*Geographers use PLACE to show different natural and cultural features at each place that exists. Have you ever been to Little Rock, Arkansas, and thought that it seemed a little different from another city? That's because it is different; these different features are what make each place special. Do you know what features make your place special? Look at what features are commonplace and what features are unique in each place. Place is what makes space special.*

# of Geography

## 3. REGION

A REGION is an area with a common language, landform, government, or more. Regions are created by people and can be referred to differently in different places. For example, northwest Arkansas is a region of Arkansas with its own features, while southeastern Arkansas is another. Differences make different regions. But, regions overlap with other regions. For example, America's Cornbelt and Wheatbelt are different regions that overlap each other. Rice is a significant export grown in our state and is produced across a region called the Ricebelt of Arkansas.

Rice fields, Eastern Arkansas

## 4. MOVEMENT

Have you ever wondered how that fresh banana arrived at your table in Arkansas all the way from Central America? It was brought in because we want it here but cannot grow it. In geography, MOVEMENT refers to the movement of people, goods, and ideas. All of these things can move from place to place. People can interact with each other through travel or trade—and even electronically through the Internet or phones. Movement is important because it explains how things change in space—throughout the house, town, state, or world! Understanding how, where, what, who, and why we move is considered an important aspect of geography.

## 5. HUMANS and the ENVIRONMENT

The relationship between HUMANS and the ENVIRONMENT includes the way people use and change the land, and how the land around us can change and influence us. For example, people build dams to control the flow of water, but the stored water can flood the reservoir behind it or the people living downstream. Humans can control parts of nature, but nature often controls us, too. So the relationship between the environment and humans is always growing and changing. In geography, understanding this sensitive and vital relationship is at the heart of creating and maintaining sustainable life and culture on our beautiful planet.

**DYK?**

There are more than 500,000 bridges longer than 20 feet in the U.S.

Bridge across the Arkansas River

**In Arkansas and across the central U.S.,
archaeologists have grouped early human residents into four distinct periods.**

The **Paleo-Indian Era** represents the arrival of the first Native Americans in the area, who arrived around 13,500 years ago at the end of the Ice Age.

The **Archaic Era** was about 9500 BC to 650 BC. Archaic peoples adapted to the warming that followed the Ice Age and the beginning of the environmental conditions we experience today. Populations grew and natural resources increased, which gave rise to sedentary living arrangements. Diverse of local plant species were domesticated toward the end of this period using innovative and widespread farming practices.

Following is the **Woodland Period**, from about 600 BC to AD 1000. This period represents the expansion of communities and economies, based on a mixture of hunting, gathering, and agriculture. It is during this era that we see the development of the bow and arrow, and fired clay pottery. Defined clans, cultures, and leadership developed during this time as well.

*Head pot from the Nodena Site near Wilson, Arkansas; circa 1550.*

Finally, the region's largest communities developed during the **Mississippi Era** (AD 900-1600) in Arkansas. Temple mounds and ceremonial centers grew around villages. These extensive communities, including Caddo settlements, were driven by economies built on craft specialization and agricultural production of corn, squash, and beans.

Archaic Era

Woodland Period

9500 BC ·········································································································· 600 BC ································································

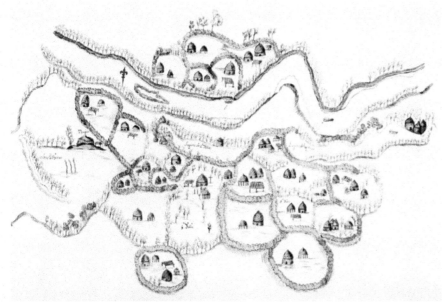

**Caddo civilization goes back more than 1,000 years before the beginning of written history.**

The Caddo Indians were farmers able to grow extensive crops of corn, beans, squash, tobacco, and sunflowers. Both men and women worked in the fields. Not only were they excellent farmers but were fine hunters as well. Bears and buffalo were hunted mainly for fat during the winter months. They also hunted deer, prairie chickens, ducks, turkeys, rabbits, mice, and snakes, in addition to fishing.

Most Caddo clothing was made from tanned deerskins with fringed decorations made with small white seeds sewn on. The Caddo were also known for their houses—pointed, thatched circular structures were characteristic of the Caddo. While the Caddo communities were self-sufficient, they carried on extensive trade with the Indians to their west. The Caddo traded bow wood for cotton blankets and turquoise from the Southwest.

Although the Caddo societies were disrupted by epidemics, they remained the most productive, advanced, and populous people of the region well into the seventeenth century.

*The first Europeans to meet the Caddo were members of the Spanish De Soto Expedition of 1542. They did not stay long in Arkansas, and more than 100 years would pass before any Europeans would return. In between, the Caddo faced extensive change. The Spaniards returned to establish missions and trading posts with the rival French colonies. Diseases like smallpox regularly ravaged Caddo communities, killing thousands. This is the part of Caddo history that enters our written history. Early chronicles mentioned more than twenty independent Caddo groups, some speaking separate dialects of a common language.*

*The Caddo Nation would later become a confederacy of many Native American tribes across the U.S. Southeast who originally inhabited much of what is now Texas, Louisiana, Oklahoma, and Arkansas. Today, the Caddo Nation Tribe is centered in Binger, Oklahoma.*

| Woodland Period | Mississippi Era | early contact | Colonization | Anglo Conflict | Resettlement |
|---|---|---|---|---|---|
| ·····AD 1000······ | | ······1542···· | ····1730······1800····· | ····1868····· | |

## ARKANSAS'S EARLY HISTORY

In 1673, French explorers Louis Joliet and Father Jacques Marquette traveled down the Mississippi River to the mouth of the Arkansas River where they were warned by the Quapaw Indians that the Indians to the south were hostile. The early explorers were thankful for the advice and turned back. Then in 1682, René-Robert Cavelier, Sieur de La Salle reached the Arkansas River on his way to the mouth of the Mississippi River. Here he visited a Quapaw village and claimed the land in the name of King Louis XIV. In 1686, Henri de Tonti founded Arkansas Post, at the confluence of the Arkansas and Mississippi rivers, the first European settlement in the lower Mississippi River Valley. It served as an important trading post and the home of a Catholic Jesuit mission.

## LOUISIANA PURCHASE, 1803

Negotiated between the U.S. under President Thomas Jefferson and France under Napoleon Bonaparte in 1803, the Louisiana Purchase was 828,800 square miles or 2,147,000 square kilometers of French territory called Louisiane, costing 60 million francs ($11,250,000). It also included the cancellation of debts worth 18 million francs ($3,750,000) for a total cost of $15,000,000. It encompassed parts of what are now 14 states and two Canadian provinces.

*After the sale, Napoleon Bonaparte said, "This accession of territory affirms forever the power of the United States, and I have given England a maritime rival who will humble her pride."*

## THE REMOVAL of the FIVE CIVILIZED TRIBES, 1830–1839

*The Five Civilized Tribes* was the term applied to five Native American nations: Cherokee, Chickasaw, Choctaw, Creek, and Seminole. These Native American tribes were considered "civilized" by early Anglo-American settlers because they adopted many of the colonists' customs and had good relations with their transplanted neighbors. These five tribes lived in the southeastern U.S. and were often forcibly relocated to other parts of the U.S., especially the future state of Oklahoma. The relocation occurred during a series of removals, authorized by the U.S. government over several decades. The most infamous removal came to be called the Trail of Tears, when President Martin Van Buren enforced the controversial Treaty of New Echota with the Cherokee Nation to exchange their property for land farther west.

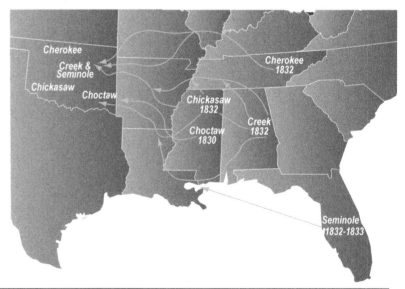

## CIVIL WAR, 1861–1865

The Civil War began after the secession of southern slave states from the U.S. Led by Jefferson Davis, the Confederate States of America fought against President Abraham Lincoln and the Union, which included all free states and four bordering slave states. Many states seceded from the Union before Lincoln took office on March 4, 1861. Arkansas seceded in May 1861. The Civil War's largest battle west of the Mississippi was fought at Pea Ridge in March 1862—a battle involving 25,000 soldiers. The Union eventually stopped Confederate advances into Missouri. In December 1862, more than 11,000 Confederate soldiers battled the Union army at Prairie Grove but failed to keep Union forces from occupying Fort Smith. Control of the Arkansas River was vital, so 30,000 Union troops successfully overtook 5,000 Confederate soldiers at Arkansas Post in January 1863, followed by the Union win at the Battle of Helena on July 4, 1863. Finally, the Union forces occupied Little Rock on September 10, 1863, so Arkansas's Confederate government was forced to relocate its capital to the town of Washington. Early in 1864, 13,000 Union troops marched from Little Rock to take over southern Arkansas, but the Red River Campaign was a failure. The Confederates ultimately surrendered in 1865.

## BROOKS-BAXTER WAR, 1874

This was not a true war but a dispute over the 1872 gubernatorial election. In the election, two Republicans, Joseph Brooks and Elisha Baxter, ran against each other. It was reported that the election was "too close to call" with Baxter finally announced as the winner. The state Supreme Court ruled against a lawsuit filed by Brooks, but Brooks won a second lawsuit filed in Pulaski County. In April 1874, Brooks was certified as the new governor; he then forcibly removed Governor Baxter from his office. Both men and their supporters appealed to the U.S. Congress and President Ulysses Grant, but the struggle escalated to gunfire and bloodshed at the Little Rock capitol. President Grant intervened, supporting Governor Baxter, but only after many confrontations and perhaps as many as 200 dead.

## DISCOVERY of BAUXITE, 1887

Bauxite is an expensive, rare ore from which aluminum is made, and it was discovered in great abundance in Arkansas in 1887. The mines produced enough ore to supply the U.S. military during WWI and WWII, helping to win the wars. The need for aluminum was so great before WWII that the annual Arkansas production of 371,000 tons jumped to 6,000,000 tons by 1943. The mining company Alcoa provided plants and mills and erected a large community near the mines.

## GREAT FLOOD of 1927

The flood was the most destructive and expensive disaster in U.S. history—6,600 square miles flooded. More than 350,000 people and 2,000,000 acres of farmland were affected, and more than 40,000 families received relief. In Arkansas, nearly 100 people died, with losses of more than $1 million in 1927. The Mississippi River remained at flood stage for 153 days.

FLOODED AREA

## DESEGREGATION OF LITTLE ROCK CENTRAL HIGH SCHOOL

In the wake of the federal *Brown v. Board of Education* decision that deemed school segregation unconstitutional, in September 1957, nine African-American students—who became known as the Little Rock Nine—began a tumultuous school year at Central High School in Little Rock. Local opposition to the desegregation of the formerly all-white school meant that the Little Rock Nine had to be accompanied by U.S. Army and federalized National Guard soldiers, and the events were covered extensively by the national media. For the following school year, known as the Lost Year, Little Rock's high schools closed rather than desegregate.

| Bauxite | Diamonds | WWI | Flood | Depression | WWII | Little Rock Desegregation Crisis | President Bill Clinton |
|---------|----------|-----|-------|------------|------|----------------------------------|------------------------|
| 1887 | 1906 | | 1927 | | 1940s | 1957 | 1990s |

Arkansas has a diverse population, from its original Native Americans to its international immigrants. From early European settlers to the multi-ethnic enclaves across Arkansas, many cultures and societies are represented. With an estimated population of 1,000 in 1810, to 1.3 million in 1900, Arkansas's population is now about 2.9 million residents. It is estimated that Arkansas will exceed 3,000,000 residents in the next few years!

*Little Rock has the highest population density in Arkansas at nearly 1,600 people per square mile.*

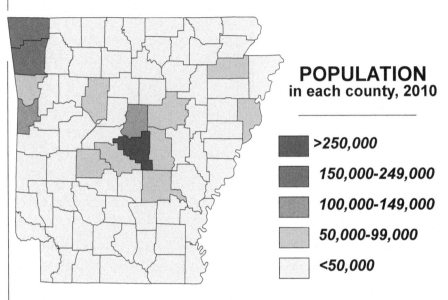

## POPULATION
### in each county, 2010

- >250,000
- 150,000-249,000
- 100,000-149,000
- 50,000-99,000
- <50,000

*The Delta, Coastal Plain, and foothills represent some of the lowest population densities in our state.*

## POPULATION DENSITY
**people per square mile in each county, 2010**

- 490
- 181 to 489
- 116 to 180
- 71 to 115
- 46 to 70
- 8 to 45

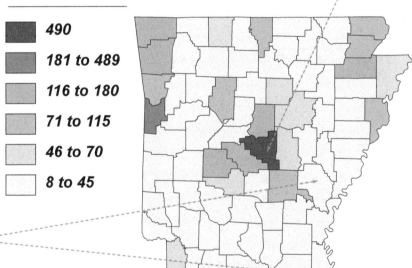

*Population density is often a better measure than population alone since it represents the number of people living in an area (in people per square mile or square kilometer). The highest density in Arkansas is in Little Rock at about 1,600 people for each square mile (2010). The average population density for our planet is 34 people per square mile, while crowded countries and cities can be much higher. The densest country on Earth is Monaco at 43,000 people per square mile, and Mongolia has the lowest density at 4 people per square mile.*

**Choropleth maps (like this one and the one above) represent one type of thematic map. They are used to portray area data (like county populations) at this scale. The color or shade represents the changing values.**

# Demography

According to the U.S. Census Bureau, the Earth's population reached 6.5 billion people on February 24, 2006. The United Nations calculated that on October 12, 1999, our planet's total population reached 6 billion. This was only 12 years after the world population reached 5 billion in 1987, and 6 years after world population reached 5.5 billion in 1993—so our population is growing FASTER and FASTER. However, the population of some countries, such as Nigeria and China, are not even known, so estimating the Earth's human population within one or two million is nearly impossible.

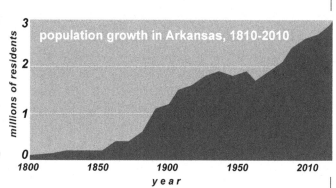

*population growth in Arkansas, 1810-2010*

**Demography is the study of the characteristics of a population, and the term "demographics" describes categories that include race, income, gender, age, disabilities, education, home ownership, location, and employment.**

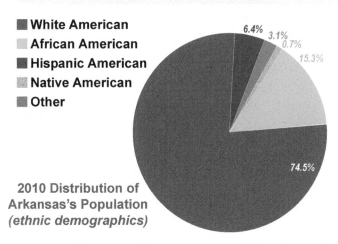

- White American
- African American
- Hispanic American
- Native American
- Other

6.4%  3.1%  0.7%  15.3%

74.5%

**2010 Distribution of Arkansas's Population**
*(ethnic demographics)*

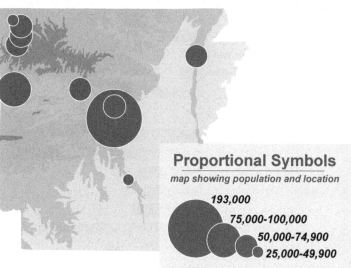

## Proportional Symbols
*map showing population and location*

193,000
75,000-100,000
50,000-74,900
25,000-49,900

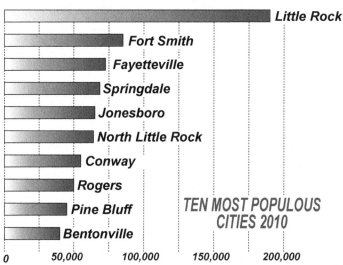

- Little Rock
- Fort Smith
- Fayetteville
- Springdale
- Jonesboro
- North Little Rock
- Conway
- Rogers
- Pine Bluff
- Bentonville

*TEN MOST POPULOUS CITIES 2010*

0  50,000  100,000  150,000  200,000

*Graduated circle maps represent one type of proportional symbol mapping. These types of thematic maps are widely used to portray point data (like city populations) at this scale. The circle size is related to the value on the map so the larger circle or symbol represents the larger value; the biggest city here (Little Rock) is represented by the biggest circle.*

Industry provides services or goods. It is a general term for any kind of production, and industry comprises four separate sectors. The primary sector is mostly raw material extraction such as mining, logging, and farming. The secondary sector involves refining, construction, and manufacturing. The third (or tertiary) sector deals with consumer services such as retail, entertainment, tourism, and personal services (like your dry cleaner or hairdresser). The fourth (or quaternary) sector is a relatively new type focused on services relating to businesses like banking, accounting, and advertising, and the fifth (or quinary) sector involves information services such as education, software development, and communications.

*Mining was one of Arkansas's largest industries in the past, and is now growing again with the extraction of natural gas across the state.*

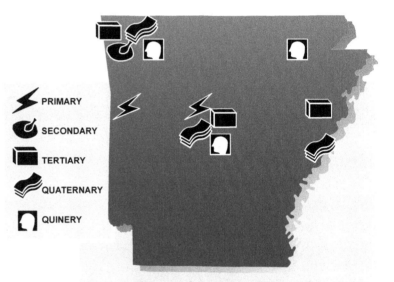

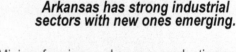

PRIMARY

SECONDARY

TERTIARY

QUATERNARY

QUINERY

**Businesses with:**

| | |
|---|---|
| 1 to 99 employees | 43,000 |
| 100 to 499 employees | |
| 500 to 999 employees | |
| 1,000 to 1,499 employees | |
| 1,500 to 2,500 employees | |
| >2,500 employees | |

NUMBER of BUSINESSES

0    500    1000

**Businesses with:**

| | |
|---|---|
| 1 to 99 employees | 346,000 |
| 100 to 499 employees | 131,000 |
| 500 to 999 employees | |
| 1,000 to 1,499 employees | |
| 1,500 to 2,500 employees | |
| >2,500 employees | 387,000 |

NUMBER of EMPLOYEES

0   20,000  40,000  60,000  80,000

**Businesses with:**

| |
|---|
| 1 to 99 employees |
| 100 to 499 employees |
| 500 to 999 employees |
| 1,000 to 1,499 employees |
| 1,500 to 2,500 employees |
| >2,500 employees |

ANNUAL WAGES PAID

0    $1 billion    $2 billion    $3 billion    $4 billion

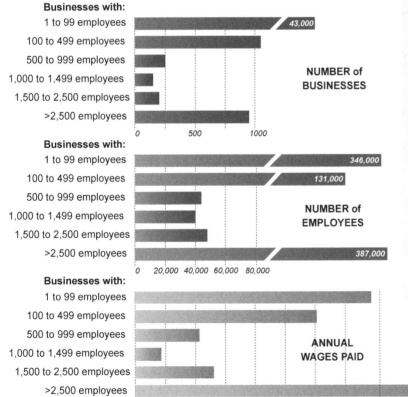

### Arkansas has strong industrial sectors with new ones emerging.

Mining, farming, and energy production are large employers and producers in the state in the ***primary (1st)*** sector.

Construction and manufacturing remain strong in the ***secondary (2nd)*** sector (Maytag, Tyson).

Arkansas retailers dominate the ***tertiary (3rd)*** sector (Wal-Mart, Dillard's, Harp's).

The ***quaternary (4th)*** sector involves Arkansas banking (Arvest).

Healthcare dominates the ***quinary (5th)*** sector (Mercy, St. Bernards, Baptist).

# ARKANSAS'S LARGEST EMPLOYERS, 2008–2009

As you can see from the horizontal bar graph above, Arkansas's industry is focused on the specific sectors of *FOOD, HEALTH, BANKING, RETAIL, and ENERGY.*

* **ENERGY** (Entergy) represents the **primary** sector
* **FOOD** (Tyson) represents the **secondary** sector
* **RETAIL** (Wal-Mart, Dillard's, Harp's) represents the **tertiary** sector
* **BANKING** (Arvest) represents the **quaternary** sector
* **HEALTH** (Mercy, St. Bernard, Baptist) represents the **quinary** sector

*Business Locations in Arkansas*

Politics is the term that involves the activities and processes involved in directing a political entity such as a nation, a state, or a local government. In democratic societies like the U.S., these entities use legislative and administrative bodies to create and enact public policies and allocate resources through a process of discussion among elected or appointed members of those bodies. Examples of such decision-making groups are a Senate, a House of Representatives, courts, and administrative agencies like the I.R.S. or departments like the U.S. Department of Education.

*Arkansas is only one of twenty-one states to have produced a president; Virginia had eight and Ohio had seven. In addition, our state has produced twelve presidential contenders including past governors Bill Clinton and Mike Huckabee.*

## William Jefferson (Bill) Clinton
### (1946 –)

*Bill Clinton was born in Hope, Arkansas. He was the 42nd president of the United States, from 1993 to 2001, and Clinton presided over the longest period of economic expansion in American history during a peacetime era. After graduating from Yale Law School, he returned to Arkansas to become a law professor at the University of Arkansas. In 1974, he ran for the House of Representatives and lost. He was then elected governor of Arkansas in 1978, making him the youngest governor in the country at 32 years old. As governor, he significantly improved Arkansas's economy and educational system. He finished his presidency with a balanced national budget, a surplus of $559 billion, and with an approval rating at 66%, the highest rating of any president leaving office since World War II. His wife, Hillary Rodham Clinton, was a U.S. senator from New York, elected in 2000, until she was appointed as the U.S. secretary of state by President Barack Obama in 2008.*

## James William (Bill) Fulbright
### (1905 – 1995)

*Bill Fulbright was born in Sumner, Missouri, and studied at Oxford University as a Rhodes Scholar. He was a lecturer in law at the University of Arkansas from 1936 to 1939 and was appointed president of the school in 1939, making him the youngest university president in the U.S. Fulbright was a Democratic senator and strong "multilateralist" who supported the establishment of the UN. He established an international exchange program, which would later bear his name as the Fulbright Fellowships.*

## Dale Leon Bumpers
### (1925 –)

*Dale Bumpers was born in Charleston, Arkansas, and was governor from 1971 to 1975. He served in the U.S. Senate from 1975 until his retirement in 1999. He defeated Senator Fulbright in 1974, and like past governors Clinton and Pryor, he was considered a strong reformer. He currently works for the law firm of Arent Fox in Washington DC.*

## Hattie Ophelia Wyatt Caraway
### (1878 – 1950)

*Hattie Caraway became the first elected woman senator in 1932. She was appointed following her husband's death in 1931 but was subsequently elected to the post. She was from Jonesboro, Arkansas, and lost her bid for reelection in 1944 to the young Bill Fulbright.*

## Michael Dale Huckabee
### (1955 –)

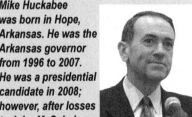

*Mike Huckabee was born in Hope, Arkansas. He was the Arkansas governor from 1996 to 2007. He was a presidential candidate in 2008; however, after losses to John McCain in Texas, Ohio, Vermont, and Rhode Island, Huckabee left the race. He is an author, a Southern Baptist minister, a musician, and a political commentator.*

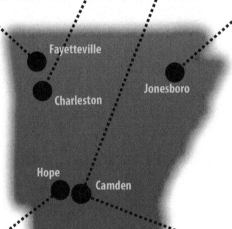

**Arkansas Politicians on the National Stage**

Fayetteville
Charleston
Jonesboro
Hope
Camden

## David Hampton Pryor
### (1934 –)

*David Pryor was born in Camden, Arkansas. He was the governor of Arkansas from 1975 to 1979, and a Democratic member of the U.S. House of Representatives from 1966 to 1973, and Senate from 1979 to 1997. He was the inaugural dean of the UA Clinton School of Public Service in Little Rock and remains active in academia and politics. His son Mark is a U.S. senator.*

## Significant Moments in ARKANSAS POLITICS

**1803** Louisiana Purchase brought in explorers and settlers who displaced the Caddo, Osage, and Quapaw Indians.

**1819** The Missouri Territory divided, creating the Arkansas Territory; Missouri then became a state in 1821.

**1836** Arkansas became the 25th U.S. state.

**1850s** Politics was dominated by the Johnson-Conway-Sevier families during the Mexican War, the California Gold Rush, and the State Bank bankruptcy.

**1861** During the Civil War, Arkansas joined the Confederacy and sustained severe loss of lives, homes, and property with nearly 4,000 Arkansans dead. The slave population was freed and began to play an important role in politics during the Reconstruction Era.

**1874** The Brooks-Baxter War was fought due to a dispute over the 1872 Arkansas gubernatorial election.

**1880s** After Reconstruction, segregation laws (e.g., poll taxes) restricted African Americans from political influence.

**1920s** The Progressive Era brought improvements in education and health. After WWI, Arkansas developed a conservative stance, even though progressive senator Joe T. Robinson became the vice-presidential candidate for the Democratic Party in 1928.

**1930s and '40s** The Great Depression destroyed Arkansas's economy, but World War II rejuvenated it.

**1957** Desegregation at Central High School in Little Rock polarized state politics, garnering national attention.

**1960s and Beyond** After Governor Orval Faubus declined to run for a seventh term, a number of progressive governors followed, including Bill Clinton, who after nearly twelve years total as governor was elected president.

### Arkansas Presidential Candidates

**George E. Taylor (1904)** *nominated but lost to Teddy Roosevelt*
**Joseph T. Robinson (1924)** *lost nomination to John W. Davis*
**William "Coin" Harvey (1932)** *nominated but lost to FDR*
**Gerald Smith (1944, 1948)** *nominated but lost to FDR, Truman*
**Orval Faubus (1960)** *nominated but lost to Kennedy*
**Eldridge Cleaver (1968)** *nominated but lost to Nixon*
**Winthrop Rockefeller (1968)** *lost nomination to Nixon*
**Wilbur Mills (1972)** *lost nomination to George McGovern*
**Bill Clinton (1992, 1996)** *nominated twice and won both elections*
**Wesley Clark (2004)** *ran in primaries but withdrew*
**Hillary Rodham Clinton (2008)** *lost nomination to Barack Obama*
**Mike Huckabee (2008)** *lost nomination to John McCain*

Arkansas's legislature is a bicameral body composed of the Senate and the House of Representatives. The General Assembly meets at the Arkansas State Capitol in Little Rock and convenes in regular session the second Monday in January in odd-numbered years; its fiscal session is the second Monday of February every even-numbered year.

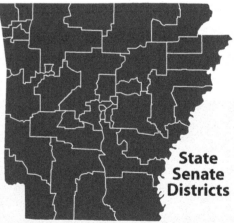

**State Senate Districts**

*The SENATE is composed of 35 members, each representing a district with roughly 76,000 people. The job of senator is a part-time job, and most senators hold a full-time job during the rest of the year. In 2010, the Senate consists of 27 Democrats and 8 Republicans; 7 senators are women and 4 are African American. Senators are elected for four-year terms with half of the Senate replaced every two years.*

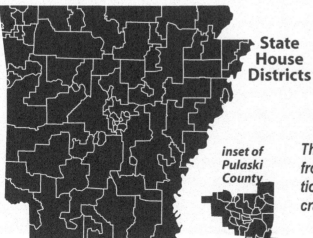

**State House Districts**

**inset of Pulaski County**

*The HOUSE of REPRESENTATIVES has 100 members elected from an equal number of constituencies with an average population of 26,734 (2000 census). In 2010, the House has 72 Democrats and 28 Republicans.*

Climatology is the study of our atmosphere's temperature, humidity, air pressure, rain and snow (precipitation), and air pollution. Climate is controlled and influenced mostly by latitude, relief (mountains and valleys), elevation, and an area's distance from large bodies of water (like oceans or lakes).

Climates can be categorized by the amount of precipitation and its distribution, in addition to temperature (highs, lows, and ranges) over time and space. Weather is the effect of climate over the short term—usually two weeks or less.

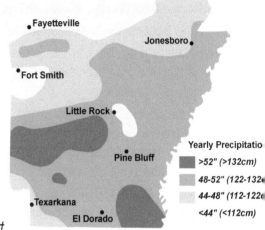

Yearly Precipitatio
- >52" (>132cm)
- 48-52" (122-132c
- 44-48" (112-122c
- <44" (<112cm)

University of Arkansas, Old Main

Ice Storm, January 2009 causing $500 million in damages!

*Our state has a temperate climate with short, cool winters and hot summers. Winters are longer and colder to the north, and summers are longer and hotter to the south. It is usually warmer and more humid in the south and the lowlands, and cooler and drier in the north, and in the mountains. In Little Rock, average daily temperatures range from 31°F (-0.6°C) lows in January to 93°F (34°C) highs in July. In Fort Smith, average lows range from 28°F (-2°C) in February to 93°F (34°C) highs in August.*

*In the Ozark and Ouachita mountains, the average annual precipitation is approximately 44–46 inches (112–117cm), but greater in the lowlands at 48–52+ inches (123–132cm). Between 1971 and 2000, Little Rock received an annual average precipitation of 51 inches (129cm), while Fort Smith received 48 inches (122cm). Snowfall averages 5–6 inches a year (12–15 cm) in Little Rock; however, on February 19, 1921, more than 18" o snow fell in Bee Branch in one day—that's the state record!*

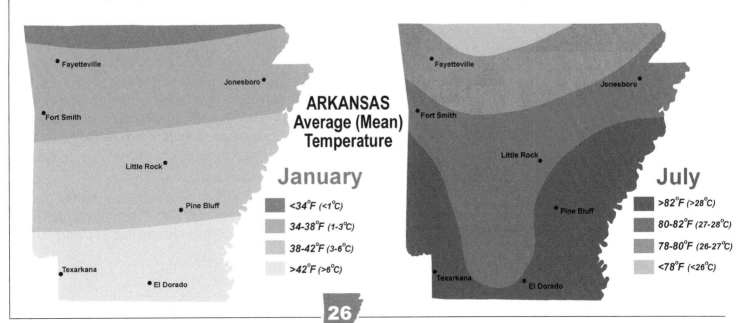

**ARKANSAS Average (Mean) Temperature**

January
- <34°F (<1°C)
- 34-38°F (1-3°C)
- 38-42°F (3-6°C)
- >42°F (>6°C)

July
- >82°F (>28°C)
- 80-82°F (27-28°C)
- 78-80°F (26-27°C)
- <78°F (<26°C)

Hot Springs National Park has some of the warmest waters in Arkansas—the water can reach 147° Fahrenheit! A hot spring is simply water that has been heated by the earth. Sometimes when pressure builds up beneath the earth, these springs throw a jet of hot water or steam into the air called a geyser. Many people visit these springs because the hot water dissolves minerals into the water that can have a healing effect on the body.

## DYK?

These hot springs were known by our area's native peoples, but the area was later established as a tourist spot in the 1880s. Some of the waters are believed to be 4,000 years old and can contain healthful healing minerals, but also harmful bacteria that can thrive in the hot water.

**Hot Springs**
★

*Hot water bubbling from the rock*

*Hot Springs' Bathhouse Row*

BUCKSTAFF

**BUCKSTAFF**
BATH HOUSE COMPANY
ARKANSAS HOT SPRINGS

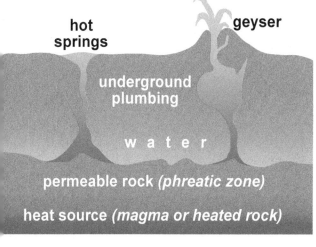

hot springs    geyser

underground plumbing

w a t e r

permeable rock *(phreatic zone)*

heat source *(magma or heated rock)*

*In regions on Earth where we see volcanoes or geothermal activity, percolated water from the atmosphere becomes heated when it comes into contact with hot magma below the surface. This can cause the water to become so hot that it boils and rushes to the surface as bubbling hot springs. Some areas do not have volcanoes, but if the water travels deep enough into the Earth, it can come into contact with hot rocks that heat up the water where it can then emerge at the surface as a steam vent, geyser, or hot spring.*

Agriculture developed about 10,000 years ago and expanded quickly due to practices like the use of fertilizers, pesticides, irrigation, and crop rotation. It is believed to have changed human history since it shifted hunting and gathering to a new focus on domesticating plants as crops and animals as livestock.

When farmers were able to grow food beyond the needs of their own families, others in their society were now free to dedicate themselves to work other than raising food. Many scholars have argued that it was agriculture that initiated civilization.

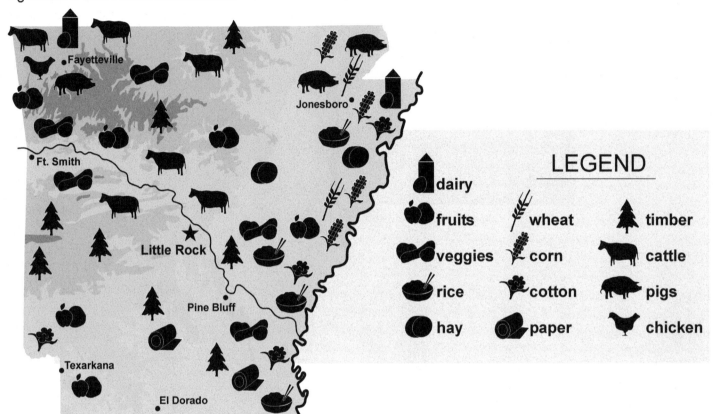

LEGEND

dairy
fruits  wheat  timber
veggies  corn  cattle
rice  cotton  pigs
hay  paper  chicken

*Agriculture is Arkansas's top source of revenue. There are more than 47,000 farms in Arkansas, and we have more than 33.3 million acres of land dedicated to agriculture. That makes agriculture very important to our state, our society, and the quality of our lives.*

## DYK?

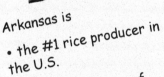

Arkansas is

- the #1 rice producer in the U.S.
- the #2 producer of chickens and the #2 producer of eggs.
- the #3 producer of turkeys and the #3 producer of aquaculture like catfish.  ... wow!

*wheat*

*rice*

*soybeans*

# in Arkansas

Agriculture is the production of food, goods, or services through farming and forestry. It is Arkansas's largest money maker, and, since our climate is varied, our crops are also diverse. We produce abundant crops in rice, wheat, barley, oats, soybeans, hay, and cotton, in addition to a thriving meat industry that includes poultry (turkey, chicken, eggs), pigs (pork, bacon, ham), cattle, dairy (milk, butter), fish, lamb, and goats. Trees, lumber, and paper also represent large businesses—this is called silviculture.

CHICKEN
(Gallus gallus)

PIG
(Sus scrofa domesticus)

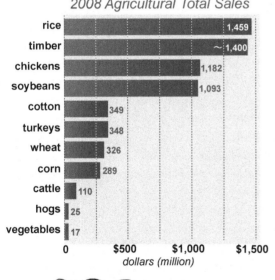

2008 Agricultural Total Sales

| | dollars (million) |
|---|---|
| rice | 1,459 |
| timber | ~1,400 |
| chickens | 1,182 |
| soybeans | 1,093 |
| cotton | 349 |
| turkeys | 348 |
| wheat | 326 |
| corn | 289 |
| cattle | 110 |
| hogs | 25 |
| vegetables | 17 |

STEER (calf)
(Bos primigenius)

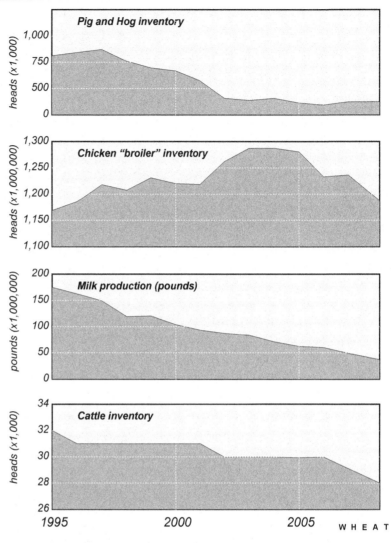

Pig and Hog inventory — heads (x1,000)

Chicken "broiler" inventory — heads (x1,000,000)

Milk production (pounds) — pounds (x1,000,000)

Cattle inventory — heads (x1,000)

WHEAT

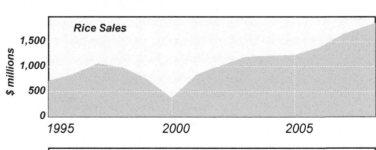

Rice Sales — $ millions

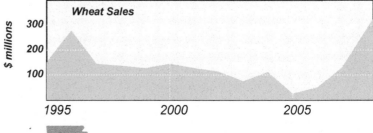

Wheat Sales — $ millions

29

Karst is a term used to describe landscapes formed from the dissolving of soluble rocks like limestone, dolomite, and gypsum, and the northern part of Arkansas is a karst region. These areas are characterized by caves, sinkholes, and underground rivers and streams (underground drainage). Most karst features on the surface are formed by internal drainage, subsidence, and collapse triggered by the development of caves beneath the surface.

*When rainwater mixes with acids produced from decaying plants, it becomes acidic and drains into fractures in the rock; the water slowly dissolves the rock. This dissolution can create a network of caves, passages, and subterranean chambers. As the water flows, it erodes and enlarges the passages, which allows this "plumbing" to transport more and more water over time. So, in karst landscapes, dissolution will lead to the development and enlargement of the caves, sinkholes, springs, and sinking streams.*

*Most Arkansans in the Ozarks get their drinking water from the karst landscape of the Ozark Plateau—a limestone plateau deposited in an ancient sea 300–400 million years ago. Under-standing our karst region is vital to our lives, especially as the population increases, because as rain falls and travels though the karst networks of caves and streams, pollutants can pass through these underground passages as well. Also, since surface runoff in karst areas does not go through natural filtering from soil layers, it leaves the aquifer especially vulnerable to contamination of artificial (chemical toxins) and natural (livestock feces) pollutants.*

*This pendant is made of banded aragonite, a mineral deposit found in caves. Many cave-deposited minerals like calcite and aragonite are polished for jewelry and decorative use.*

*The minerals can display banded beige, orange, white, and brown colors.*

*Cave deposits like speleothems, however, are fragile and should not be handled.*

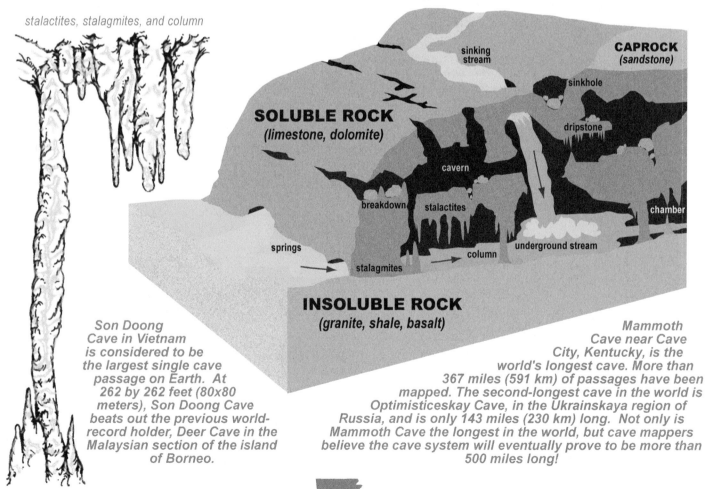

*stalactites, stalagmites, and column*

SOLUBLE ROCK
*(limestone, dolomite)*

sinking stream

CAPROCK
*(sandstone)*

sinkhole

dripstone

cavern

breakdown

stalactites

chamber

springs

column

underground stream

stalagmites

INSOLUBLE ROCK
*(granite, shale, basalt)*

*Son Doong Cave in Vietnam is considered to be the largest single cave passage on Earth. At 262 by 262 feet (80x80 meters), Son Doong Cave beats out the previous world-record holder, Deer Cave in the Malaysian section of the island of Borneo.*

*Mammoth Cave near Cave City, Kentucky, is the world's longest cave. More than 367 miles (591 km) of passages have been mapped. The second-longest cave in the world is Optimisticeskay Cave, in the Ukrainskaya region of Russia, and is only 143 miles (230 km) long. Not only is Mammoth Cave the longest in the world, but cave mappers believe the cave system will eventually prove to be more than 500 miles long!*

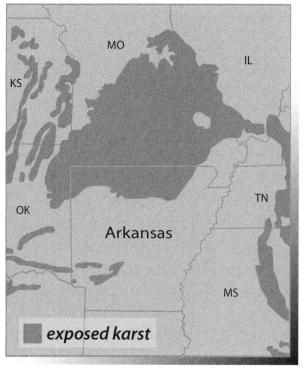

**exposed karst**

## NOTABLE CAVES in ARKANSAS

**ONYX CAVE** is located about six miles east of Eureka Springs and has been a tourist attraction since 1893, making it the oldest "show" cave in Arkansas. The cave contains a beautiful kind of flowstone called cave onyx that shows bands of different colors. Many of the strangely shaped speleothems include the Friendly Dragon, Witches' Fireplace, and Lion's Head. The cave holds a consistent temperature of 57°F (14°C) year round.

**COSMIC CAVERN** is located near Berryville and has been advertised as "Arkansas's Most Beautifully Decorated Cave." The cave has an abundance of speleothems including stalactites, stalagmites, flowstone, cave popcorn, cave bacon, and soda straws. One section of the cave has an especially spectacular display of soda straws and is touted as "Silent Splendor." The longest soda straw formation hangs nine feet in length. Cosmic Cavern has two "bottomless" lakes since cave divers have never found the bottoms. The south lake was stocked with trout in the 1920s, and over the years these fish have become blind and have lost all color. Other life in the cave includes the endemic Ozark Blind Cave Salamander. This cave is considered the warmest in the Ozarks with a constant 62°F (17°C) year-round temperature.

**MYSTIC CAVERNS and CRYSTAL DOME** (called the Twin Caves) are located between Jasper and Harrison and have operated commercially since the late 1920s. Crystal Dome was discovered in the mid-1960s, although tours did not begin until 1981. These caves contain more speleothems per foot than any other caves in Arkansas and maintain a consistent year-round temperature of 58°F (14°C). There is a third cave on the site called Not Much Sink Cavern, but it is considered too dangerous to allow public access.

**OLD SPANISH TREASURE CAVE** is located near Gravette and has a legendary history. It is believed that Spanish conquistadors hid gold in caves before they were killed or returned to Spain. Although no gold was ever found, Spanish helmets, weapons, and pieces of armor were discovered. The cave was opened in the 1930s, and the hunt for the treasure has been ongoing, as the cave has never been fully explored. The cave stays at a constant 56°F (13°C) all year.

**BLANCHARD SPRINGS CAVERNS** is a three-level cave system north of Mountain View. Locals knew about the caves since the 1930s, but mapping and exploration did not begin until 1955 when a 1,000-year-old Native American skeleton was found. The caverns opened to the public in 1973 after ten years of development on the Dripstone Trail (cave's upper level). The Discovery Trail was opened in 1977 (middle level). The cave is considered "living" because speleothems continue to grow and change through the slow movement of seeping mineral-laden water. The caverns remain at a constant 58°F (14°C) year round.

Mystic Caverns

Blanchard Springs Caverns

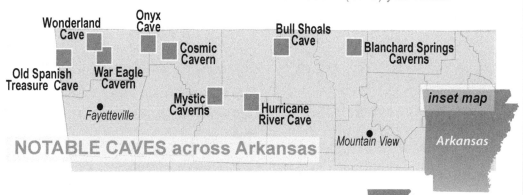

Wonderland Cave

Onyx Cave

Bull Shoals Cave

Blanchard Springs Caverns

Cosmic Cavern

Old Spanish Treasure Cave

War Eagle Cavern

Mystic Caverns

Hurricane River Cave

Fayetteville

Mountain View

inset map

Arkansas

NOTABLE CAVES across Arkansas

## DYK?

Minerals represent some of the most valuable things on earth: gemstones. For example, the "Millennium Star" diamond weighs 203 carats and is worth more than $150,000,000 (or about $750,000 per carat). It's roughly the size and weight of a large walnut! Also, an 8.62 carat ruby recently sold for $3,660,000 or about $425,000 per carat. Few objects so small are worth so much!

*"Millennium Star" diamond*
------
*203.04 carats*

A mineral is a naturally occurring material that is formed through geologic processes. A mineral must have distinctive chemical composition, atomic structure, and physical properties. The study of minerals is called mineralogy. Minerals range in composition from pure elements (like a gold nugget or a diamond crystal that is pure carbon) to complex silicates with thousands of forms (like tourmaline or mica).

A rock, by comparison, is an aggregate of minerals and does not have to have a specific chemical composition. For example, granite is a rock and is a mixture of minerals like quartz, mice, feldspar, and hornblende. The study of rocks is called petrology while the study of the Earth and its materials is called geology.

*The processes that change our planet are measured in very different scales, like minutes for earthquakes or avalanches; hours or days for floods; decades for glacier advance or retreat; centuries for soil development, called pedogenesis; and millions of years for rock formation, called lithification.*

### GEOLOGIC TIMELINE
million years ago

| | |
|---|---|
| **CENOZOIC** | **Holocene** (10,000 years ago) |
| | **Pleistocene** (0.1 to 1.6my) |
| | **Pliocene** (1.6-5my) |
| | **Miocene** (5-24my) |
| | **Oligocene** (24-37my) |
| | **Eocene** (37-58my) |
| | **Paleocene** (58-66my) |
| **MESOZOIC** | **Cretaceous** (66-144my) |
| | **Jurassic** (144-208my) |
| | **Triassic** (208-245my) |
| **PALEOZOIC** | **Permian** (245-286my) |
| | **Pennsylvanian** (286-320my) |
| | **Mississippian** (320-360my) |
| | **Devonian** (360-406my) |
| | **Silurian** (406-438my) |
| | **Ordovician** (438-505my) |
| | **Cambrian** (505-570my) |
| | **PRECAMBRIAN** (570+my) |

*Quartz is the most common mineral on Earth, but in its rarest forms, it occurs in beautiful colors as valuable gemstones:*

**CITRINE (yellow)**

**AMETHYST (purple)**

**SMOKY (brown-gray)**

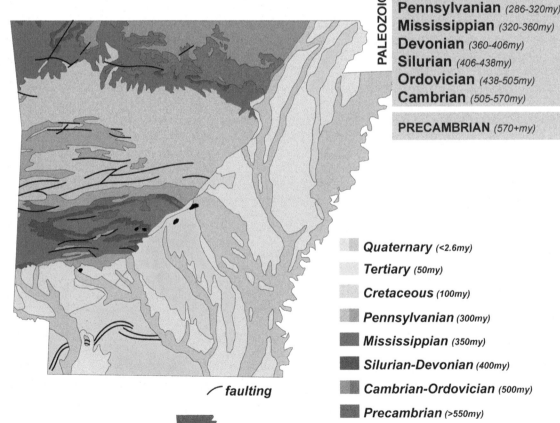

⟋ faulting

Quaternary (<2.6my)
Tertiary (50my)
Cretaceous (100my)
Pennsylvanian (300my)
Mississippian (350my)
Silurian-Devonian (400my)
Cambrian-Ordovician (500my)
Precambrian (>550my)

Mining is the process of the removal of valuable and/or useful minerals, rocks, or other geological materials from the earth, usually from a vein (like silver), an ore body (like gold), a seam (like coal), or from a massive deposit (like quarried limestone). In general, mining can be considered the extraction of any non-renewable resource (like minerals, rock material, petroleum, natural gas, or water). Mined materials in Arkansas include iron, vanadium, coal, diamonds, crushed and quarried stone, bromides, barite, quartz crystals, tripoli, gypsum, bauxite, and chalk.

## DYK?

No metals are currently mined in Arkansas, while in some states, metals (like copper in Arizona) are the primary mined materials.

These metals used to be important here but haven't been mined since 1990: Bauxite (Al), Antimony (Sb), Copper (Cu), Gallium (Ga), Iron (Fe), Lead (Pb), Manganese (Mn), Mercury (Hg), Silver (Ag), Titanium (Ti), Vanadium (V), Zinc (Zn).

**QUARTZ CRYSTAL**
*(smoky variety)*

**BROMIDE**
*("salt" chunk)*

**COAL**

**BAUXITE**
*(aluminum ore)*

FAYETTEVILLE SHALE

*Little Rock

*Natural gas is a by-product of petroleum and, less frequently, coal beds. This valuable fuel is at the center of Arkansas's newest mining boom. The Fayetteville Shale is a natural-gas-producing field that runs across the state from Fort Smith to Helena.*

*Fayetteville Shale's extent or "play" is about 60–575 feet thick, and is found 1,450–6,700 feet below the surface, taking up about 4,000 square miles! Recent studies show that it could contain 20 trillion cubic feet of gas and could generate up to $17,000,000,000 and 10,000 jobs in our state.*

*Mining techniques can be divided into two types, surface and underground, while mined materials can be divided into two categories, placer (gravels, sands, and unconsolidated) and lode (veins, beds, or layers, or in mineral grains in the rock mass). Both ores or placer*

**Open-pit coal mining in Bates, Arkansas**

*deposits can be mined at or below the surface. Placer mining uses gravity to separate the heavier ore from a liquid like water. The ore then requires crushing to extract the minerals from the surrounding rock. A third technique is used in Arkansas where bromide-rich waters are evaporated to concentrate bromine, Arkansas's biggest mined resource.*

Coal crushing in Bates, Arkansas

*In surface mining, the surface materials or "overburden" are removed above the valuable minerals. The overburden can include plants, dirt, and less valuable rock above the more valuable ore deposits or buried placer deposits. In open-pit mining, the overburden is removed by stripping off surface layers to expose the ore beneath. In underground mining, tunnels and shafts are dug into the earth to reach the ore. Horizontal tunnels are called drifts, vertical tunnels are called shafts, and removing materials to create underground rooms is called stoping.*

Diamonds are minerals composed of pure carbon in a unique atomic isometric (evenly spaced) arrangement. Although graphite (pencil "lead") has the same composition, the isometric carbons make diamonds the hardest natural substance on Earth. Since they are so resistant to scratching, diamonds are ideal for drilling, abrasives, and jewelry. The first diamonds were found in India; however, now nearly half of all diamonds are now mined in southern Africa, with other sources found in Canada, Russia, India, Australia, and Arkansas—the ONLY location in the U.S.!

### Uncle Sam Diamond

*Found by W.O. Bassum in 1924 in Murfreesboro, the stone was named the Uncle Sam. Originally weighing 40.23 carats, the diamond was faceted into an emerald-shaped stone weighing around 12.42 carats. In 1971, this rare diamond was sold for $150,000 and is now preserved in the American Museum of Natural History.*

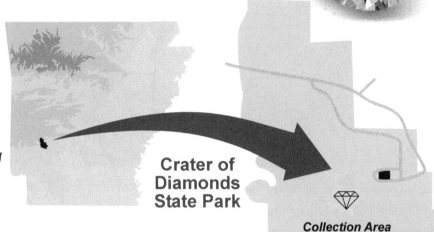

**Crater of Diamonds State Park**

**Collection Area (exposed pipe)**

John Huddleston

Crater of Diamonds is an 888-acre state park near Murfreesboro that sits atop an eroding 37-acre diamond pipe of the diamond-bearing mineral LAMPROITE. Although the first diamond was discovered in 1906, the park was not established until 1972.

The park is open to the public for collecting, and more than 600 diamonds are discovered each year. Each diamond can be kept by the finder, regardless of size, quality, or color. The first diamonds were discovered by John Huddleston in 1906 and a "diamond rush" followed. Since then, more than 100,000 diamonds have been found in Arkansas, ranging in size from tiny grains to more than 40 carats!

Other diamonds found at the park include an unnamed 20.25 carat gem, the **Arkansas Crystal** (17.85cts), the **Star of Arkansas** (15.31cts), the **Chief of Carlisle** (13.50cts), the **Colton Bell Star** (11.93cts), the **Gary Moore** (6.43cts), and the **Star of Murfreesboro** (34.25cts).

*STRAWN-WAGNER Diamond*

*Shirley Strawn found a stone in 1990 weighing 3.03 carats. It was cut into a 1.09 carat, round brilliant, D-color (colorless) internally flawless (IF) gem. It is now on display at the Crater of Diamonds Museum.*

*RODEN Diamond*

*Donald and Brenda Roden found this 6.35 carat coffee-colored diamond in 2006.*

**DIAMONDS IN PIKE**
John Huddleston Has Sold Two Stones
**AN OFFER OF $36,000**
Diamonds Were Found Has Been Refused.

# Arkansas

The Crater of Diamonds is a 95-million-year-old eroded volcano composed of lamproite, which carried diamonds from the mantle, where they developed and crystallized through the crust to the surface. Most diamonds on Earth are mined from kimberlite (like in South Africa), but the Arkansas diamonds are mined from lamproite, a related mineral that also supplies the diamonds at the Australian mines.

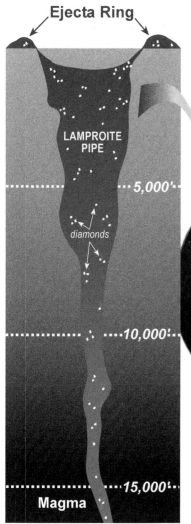

Ejecta Ring

LAMPROITE PIPE

5,000'

diamonds

10,000'

15,000'

Magma

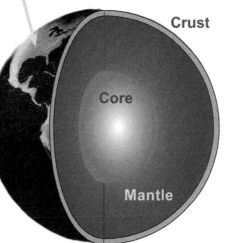

Crust

Core

Mantle

## DYK?

Diamonds can be polished to such a fine edge that they can be used in eye and nerve micro-surgery!

Blue diamonds that contain the element Boron (B) are more conductive than any other substance, even copper!

Non-jewelry-quality rough diamonds called "bort" can be used in drill bits that can grind through the hardest rocks or metals!

Colored diamonds are far more valuable than colorless ones; they can be red, blue, or golden!

The sparkle in a diamond is a function of its faceting geometry, mineral color, and its polish. This scintillation helps the light entering the stone return to the eye with flashes of color, light, and shadow.

### Popular shapes of faceted diamonds

Oval  Pear  Marquise  Emerald

Square  Asher  Heart  Round

*Diamond crystals or "rough" can be used without any change from the ground and are found in three forms (octahedron, macle, and irregular). But in jewelry like rings or pendants, diamonds are cut and then faceted to increase their natural brilliance.*

octahedron rough

macle rough

irregular rough
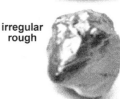

Ecosystems are the combined components of the environment that include the botanical (plants), zoological (animals), and physical (rocks, climate, soil) parts. It is an area within the natural environment in which the physical aspects function together with interdependent animals and plants, all within the same habitat.

## OZARK PLATEAU

The Ozark Plateau is a physiographic, geologic, biotic, and cultural highland region that covers nearly 47,000 square miles (122,000 km²) across Arkansas, Missouri, Oklahoma, and Kansas. It is considered the largest mountain range between the Appalachians and the Rockies. The Boston Mountains are the highest part at just over 2,560 feet (780 m) with valleys 500 to 1,550 feet deep (150 m–470 m). Turner Ward Knob is the highest named point at 2,463 feet (751 m), but nearby unnamed peaks measure 2,560 feet (780 m).

Karst features such as caves, disappearing streams, sinkholes, and springs are common in the limestone and dolomite rocks here. The Ozark forests are dominated by hardwoods including white oaks (white, post, chinquapin), oaks (red, black), hickory, sweetgum, and sugar maple while lower areas are filled with sycamore, Ozark witch hazel, elm, and other bottomland hardwood trees. Cedars are often found in unburned areas, while pines grow in acidic soils often related to subsurface sandstones. In 1908, President Teddy Roosevelt created what is now the Ozark-St. Francis National Forest. These protected areas were created for the recovery of endangered and threatened species like the Indiana and Ozark big-eared bats, Ozark cavefish, eastern small-footed bat, southeastern big-eared bat, longnose darter, Ozark cave crayfish, Bowman's and Ozark cave amphipods, bat cave isopod, and Ozark chinquapin. The Buffalo National River was created in 1972 as the nation's first National River administered by the U.S. National Park Service, which ensures protection from industrial use, damming, and other changes that may alter the natural character of the river or affect the natural habitat for the flora and fauna that live there.

**Buffalo River**

## ARKANSAS RIVER VALLEY

Dominated by the Arkansas River, the valley is flanked by the Ozark Plateau to the north and the Ouachita Mountains to the south. The valley is dominated by elm, sycamore, and bottomland hardwood trees like oak, gum, and cypress. This ecosystem can contain flowering and fruiting plants, so a variety of ground birds and songbirds may be present. Wild turkeys, woodcocks, and many ducks can be seen in these habitats in addition to woodpeckers, warblers, owls, cardinals, blue jays, and wrens. Mammals include deer, bears, wild hogs, raccoons, skunks, foxes, otters, minks, and gray squirrels. Several species of snakes live in the river valley, including coral snakes, copperheads, cottonmouths, eastern diamond-back rattlesnakes, and many non-poisonous varieties. Box and mud turtles live in the moist areas, while many frogs, skinks, and fish breed in the shallow waters and vegetation.

## OUACHITA MOUNTAINS

The Ouachita Mountains are separated from the Ozarks by the Arkansas River channel and, unlike most mountain chains in the U.S., the Ouachitas run east and west. This ecosystem contains large woodlands of stunted northern red oak, and white, post, and blackjack oak at elevations over 2,500 feet (760 m) on steep, dry slopes. On lower slopes, eastern red cedar, gum bumelia, winged elm, and yaupon may be found. Many of these forests were never logged and may total 800,000 acres (3,200 km²). Along the western edge of the Ouachita Mountains is the Ouachita National Forest, which encompasses nearly 1.8 million acres (7,200 km²). Twenty-three aquatic animals, including 12 crayfish, 8 fish, and 3 mussels, are found nowhere else on Earth but in the Ouachita Mountains. The Ouachita Mountains area is also known for its famous quartz crystals from Mount Ida.

## CROWLEY'S RIDGE

Crowley's Ridge is an unusual geological formation that rises 250 feet to 550 feet (76 m–168 m) above the alluvial plain of the delta: twelve miles (19 km) at its widest and half a mile at its narrowest. The ridge is a narrow band of rolling hills that arcs 150 miles (240 km) from southeastern Missouri to the Mississippi River near Helena.

The ridge is composed of loess, a windblown sediment, and contrasts greatly with the plain surrounding it since loess is a distinctly gray-yellow color while the Mississippi alluvial soil is dark brown to black. It is believed to have been an island between the Mississippi and Ohio rivers, which changed their courses millions of years ago. The plants and animals of these hills are more closely related to Tennessee hills (to the east) than to the Ozark Plateau (to the west), which may support this theory. Others, however, have postulated that the ridge is due to subsurface shifting and uplifting, related to the New Madrid Seismic Zone.

The ridge is forested with oak, hickory, beech, and poplar trees, in addition to numerous flowers including phlox, verbena, wild hydrangea, hibiscus, aster, jasmine, crimson catchfly, butterfly weed, cardinal flower, and blue lobelia. Interestingly, this vegetation is most similar to the flora of the Appalachian Mountains. Since the plains surrounding Crowley's Ridge were once much swampier, these rolling hills provided an ideal home for early settlers and a natural north-south corridor for travelers.

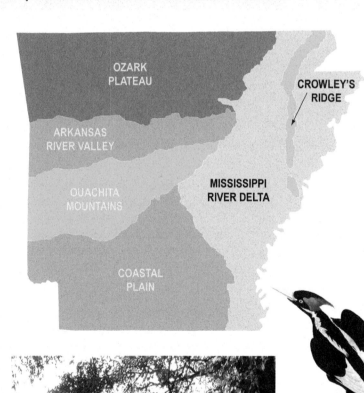

## MISSISSIPPI RIVER DELTA

Arkansas's delta runs along the eastern border with the Mississippi River as part of the Mississippi embayment and the Mississippi River alluvial plain. The region shares geographic and cultural characteristics with the Mississippi Delta on the eastern back of the river in the states of Tennessee and Mississippi.

The earliest settlers lived along the river in the swamps and bayous of east Arkansas, including the first state capital, Arkansas Post. However, Native Americans occupied the region for 12,000 years. Since its earliest days, the demographics of the delta have changed little—it still exhibits some of the lowest population densities in the South.

The regional economy is still dominated by agriculture with cotton, rice, and soybeans the primary crops across this flat landscape. In 1927, it was inundated by a great flood that submerged most of the region; however, the flood also replenished the region's alluvial plain, enriching soils and increasing productivity for years to come. In 2005, the ivory-billed woodpecker (*Campephilus principalis*) was sighted in a swamp in the area, once believed to be extinct since it was last sighted in 1944. The sighting has rekindled bird-watching tourism across Arkansas's Mississippi River Delta.

**Ivory-billed Woodpecker**
*by John James Audubon*

## COASTAL PLAIN

The coastal plain is characterized by flatland forests and farms. The railroads of the late 1800s impacted the area when lumber companies stripped many of the forests, forcing some native plant and animal species—like the red-cockaded woodpecker—nearly into extinction. The uplands are dominated by pines where bird populations include wrens, sparrows, American kestral, and the prairie warbler. The bottomlands are dominated by hardwood forests that include kites, warblers, and vireos. The discovery of petroleum and gas, bromine flats, and bauxite (aluminum ore) brought great wealth along with environmental degradation. The lowest point in Arkansas is found in the flat land of the West Gulf coastal plains where the Ouachita River enters Louisiana—55 feet above sea level.

Cave crayfish

Why do species go extinct? A habitat is the place where an animal or plant lives that has everything it needs to survive, like water, food, shelter, and space. Often, habitats are destroyed when humans change the natural landscape. Pollution, illegal killing, overcollection, and the introduction of non-native species also cause many species to become endangered.

Least interior tern

What is an endangered species? An endangered species is in immediate danger of going extinct; extinct species are no longer living on Earth. A species that is threatened is likely to become endangered if not protected. In order to protect these endangered and threatened species, the Endangered Species Act (ESA) was passed by Congress in 1973. The purpose of the ESA is to conserve and protect endangered and threatened species, as well as the ecosystems in which they live. The U.S. Fish and Wildlife Service and the National Marine Fisheries Service of the National Oceanic and Atmospheric Administration are in charge of deciding which plants and animals need to be protected.

Red-cockaded woodpecker (*Picoides borealis*)
Ouachita rock pocketbook (*Arkansia wheeleri*)
Pink mucket (*Lampsilis abrupta*)
Scaleshell mussel (*Leptodea leptodon*)
Cave crayfish (*Cambarus zophonastes*)
Cave crayfish (*Cambarus aculabrum*)
Running buffalo clover
(*Trifolium stoloniferum*)
Speckled Pocketbook (*Lampsilis streckeri*)
Indiana bat (*Myotis sodalis*)
Ozark cavefish (*Amblyopsis rosae*)
Gray wolf (*Canis lupus*)
Leopard darter (*Percina pantherina*)
Arkansas River Basin shiner (*Notropis girardi*)

Missouri bladderpod (*Lesquerella filiformis*)
Fat pocketbook (*Potamilus capax*)
Harperella (*Ptilimnium nodosum*)
No common name (*Geocarpon minimum*)
Least interior tern (*Sterna antillarum*)
Pondberry (*Lindera melissifolia*)
Eskimo curlew (*Numenius borealis*)
Florida panther (*Puma concolor coryi*)
Gray bat (*Myotis grisescens*)
Arkansas fatmucket (*Lampsilis powellii*)
Pallid sturgeon (*Scaphirhynchus albus*)
Eastern prairie fringed orchid (*Platanthera leucophaea*)
American burying beetle (*Nicrophorus americanus*)
Ivory-billed woodpecker (*Campephilus principalis*)
Ozark big-eared bat (*Corynorhinus townsendii ingens*)
Magazine Mountain shagreen (*Mesodon magazinensis*)
Curtis pearlymussel (*Epioblasma florentina curtisii*)

## 30 Protected Species in Arkansas

Eastern prairie fringed orchid

## DYK?

In Arkansas, 30 species are listed as being endangered or threatened. Of these, 24 species are animal and 6 are plant.

# Protected Lands

What are protected lands? Protected lands are, for example, national parks, nature reserves, wilderness areas, and wildlife management areas, which are areas set aside in order to conserve natural ecosystems, many of which would be destroyed by human development without protection. These areas also act as havens for wildlife and provide safe places for threatened and endangered species to repair the damage to their populations. Protected lands can be maintained at many different levels, from the government (federal, state, and local), to private organizations, to private citizens or citizen groups.

*Felsenthal National Wildlife Refuge*

*White River National Wildlife Refuge*

Protected lands are important to humans since they benefit us by maintaining biodiversity that provides safe places for wildlife to prosper. However, protected lands also provide humans with places to go to enjoy beautiful natural scenery and serve as areas for recreation (camping, hiking). Protected lands can also preserve historic sites, keeping them from being destroyed by modern development.

## The Grand Prairie Project

*A major portion of the United States' rice and soybean crops are grown in eastern Arkansas. Agriculture in this area depends heavily on water in order to irrigate crops. Presently, this area is in danger of losing access to enough water for these crops because of failing wells and depleted aquifers. A plan has been proposed to pump large amounts of water from the nearby White River in order to provide this area with additional water. Without an additional water source, this region stands to lose its largest crop. However, pumping large quantities of water away from the White River will drastically change its ecology and endanger the White River National Wildlife Refuge, which is a large, rich area of old-growth timber.*

## Protected Areas in Arkansas

Pea Ridge National Military Park
Ozark National Forest
Leatherwood Wilderness
Buffalo National River Wilderness
Ozark National Forest
Upper Buffalo Wilderness
Ozark National Forest
Richland Creek Wilderness
Big Lake National Wildlife Refuge
Chickasaw National Wildlife Refuge
Ozark National Forest
East Fork Wilderness
Hurricane Creek Wilderness
Cache River National Wildlife Refuge
Wapanocca National Wildlife Refuge
Ozark National Forest
Bald Knob National Wildlife Refuge
Cache River National Wildlife Refuge
Poteau Mountain Wilderness
Holla Bend National Wildlife Refuge
Cache River National Wildlife Refuge
Dry Creek Wilderness
Black Fork Mtn. Wilderness
Flatside Wilderness
Saint Francis National Forest
Ouachita National Forest
Hot Springs National Park
Caney Creek Wilderness
White River National Wildlife Refuge
Pond Creek National Wildlife Refuge
Felsenthal National Wildlife Refuge
Overflow National Wildlife Refuge

The Arkansas Department of Parks and Tourism (ADPT) manages fifty-two state parks and sites and promotes the state of Arkansas as a tourist destination. Petit Jean State Park was Arkansas's first park, created in 1923 by Act 276, which authorized the state to accept land donations for state parks and reservations. Arkansas, however, did not have an agency to oversee the establishment of state parks until 1927 when Act 172 was enacted to create the seven-member State Parks Commission to:

*"select and acquire such areas of the State of Arkansas which, by reason of their natural features, scenic beauty and historical interest, have educational, recreational, health, camping and out-door life advantages."*

Over the years, various commissions served until 1971 when a number of state agencies were reorganized and combined by Act 38. Then in 1996, Arkansans approved Amendment 75, which created a one-eighth-cent tax to support state agencies working on conservation issues, including the ADPT.

*Arkansas's state parks range from museums to mountains to battlefields to springs and lakes.*

| | | |
|---|---|---|
| Arkansas Museum of Natural Resources | Jenkins' Ferry State Park | Mount Nebo State Park |
| Arkansas Post Museum | Lake Catherine State Park | Ozark Folk Center State Park |
| Bull Shoals-White River State Park | Lake Charles State Park | Parkin Archeological State Park |
| Cane Creek State Park | Lake Chicot State Park | Petit Jean State Park |
| Conway Cemetery Historic State Park | Lake Dardanelle State Park | Pinnacle Mountain State Park |
| Cossatot River State Park-Natural Area | Lake Fort Smith State Park | Plantation Agriculture Museum |
| Crater of Diamonds State Park | Lake Frierson State Park | Poison Spring State Park |
| Crowley's Ridge State Park | Lake Ouachita State Park | Powhatan Courthouse State Park |
| Daisy State Park | Lake Poinsett State Park | Prairie Grove Battlefield State Park |
| Davidsonville Historic State Park | Logoly State Park | Queen Wilhelmina State Park |
| DeGray Lake Resort State Park | Louisiana Purchase State Park | South Arkansas Arboretum |
| Delta Heritage Trail State Park | Lower White River Museum State Park | Toltec Mounds Archeological State Park |
| Devil's Den State Park | Mammoth Spring State Park | Village Creek State Park |
| Hampson Museum State Park | Marks' Mills State Park | White Oak Lake State Park |
| Herman Davis State Park | Millwood State Park | Withrow Springs State Park |
| Historic Washington State Park | Mississippi River State Park | Woolly Hollow State Park |
| Hobbs State Park-Conservation Area | Moro Bay State Park | |
| Jacksonport State Park | Mount Magazine State Park | |

The Natural State is dotted with national sites as well. Hot Springs National Park is our most notable national park; however, six other U.S. National Park Service sites are located across the state. These national sites include the spectacular beauty of our nation's first national river, the first permanent European settlement in the lower Mississippi River Valley, the frontier outpost on the nation's border with the Indian Territory until 1907, an American civil rights landmark, a crucial Civil War battlefield west of the Mississippi River, and the birthplace home of President Bill Clinton.

*Arkansas's diverse national sites include the following:*

**Arkansas Post National Memorial:** *first permanent European settlement along the Mississippi*
**Buffalo National River:** *America's first nationally protected scenic river*
**Central High School National Historic Site:** *site of school desegregation battle in 1957*
**Clinton Birthplace Home National Historic Site:** *first home to our 42nd president*
**Fort Smith National Historic Site:** *site of two 19th-century military forts*
**Hot Springs National Park:** *est. in 1832; oldest national park, with hot springs and bath houses*
**Pea Ridge National Military Park:** *important Civil War battlefield of March 7-8,1862*

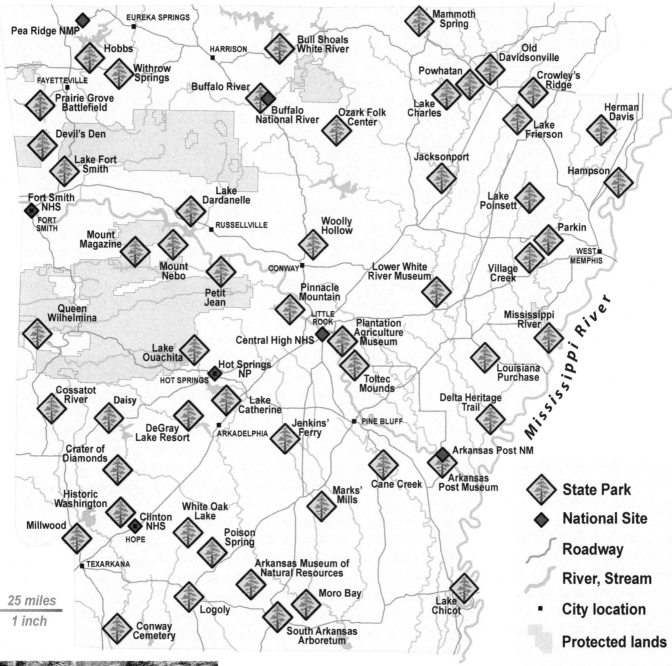

**State Park**

**National Site**

**Roadway**

**River, Stream**

**City location**

**Protected lands**

25 miles
1 inch

Cedar Falls, Petit Jean State Park

The Arkansas State Parks System was created around a four-part vision.

*(1) To provide the best recreational and educational opportunities, (2) to protect its natural, historical, and cultural resources, (3) to enhance the economy of the state by providing recreation destinations and leisure services for its visitors, and (4) to create conservation resources for Arkansas's diverse landscapes.*

Our Natural State is fortunate to have such stewardship of nature and conservation, as well as recreation, diversity, and beauty.

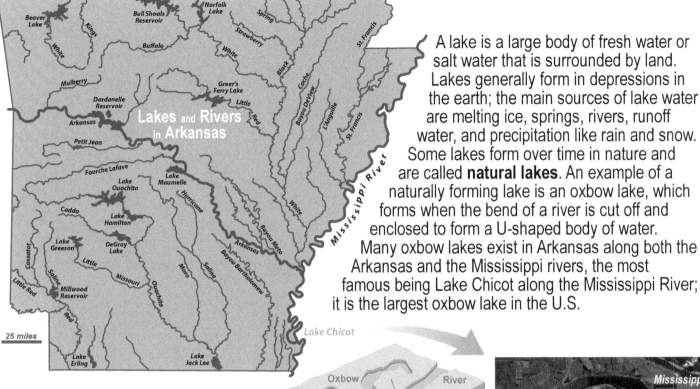

Lakes and Rivers in Arkansas

25 miles

A lake is a large body of fresh water or salt water that is surrounded by land. Lakes generally form in depressions in the earth; the main sources of lake water are melting ice, springs, rivers, runoff water, and precipitation like rain and snow. Some lakes form over time in nature and are called **natural lakes**. An example of a naturally forming lake is an oxbow lake, which forms when the bend of a river is cut off and enclosed to form a U-shaped body of water. Many oxbow lakes exist in Arkansas along both the Arkansas and the Mississippi rivers, the most famous being Lake Chicot along the Mississippi River; it is the largest oxbow lake in the U.S.

Lake Chicot

Oxbow          River

Soil is deposited

Erosion at the river bends reduces the land in between.

Lake Chicot in the southeast corner of Arkansas is the largest oxbow lake in the U.S. It is over 20 miles long, and was once part of the Mississippi River.

Mississippi River

Lake Chicot

Other lakes are designed and built by humans; these lakes are called **artificial lakes**. An artificial lake is created by flooding land behind a dam, called an impoundment or reservoir. Some of the world's largest lakes are man-made. Lake Ouachita is an example of a man-made lake. In 1955, land was flooded to form Lake Ouachita, which has a surface area of 20,900 acres, making it one of the largest lakes that exists entirely within Arkansas's borders. Trees over 60 feet tall can still be found at the bottom of the lake!

*One of the most common uses of lakes in Arkansas is recreation. Boating and fishing are common past-times, as well as sports like water and jet skiing. Lake areas are also great places to go camping, hiking, or picnicking, and to find all kinds of creatures like turtles and frogs. But lakes are invaluable to us as sources of water for drinking and irrigation.*

**DYK?**

Many of our lakes were created by flooding large areas of land. So, houses and other buildings that stand underwater serve as attractions for snorkelers and scuba divers, and as hiding places for fish and lake life.

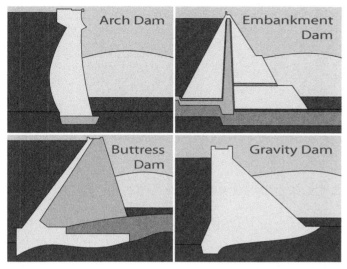

A dam is a barrier that creates water collection and storage. Many dams today are man-made, but dams can also be the result of natural events like landslides, or of wildlife like beavers. Man-made dams are measured according to their height, structure type, purpose, and storage capacity (called acre-feet).

## DYK?

One cubic yard is a measure of volume. One cubic yard of liquid is equal to about 202 gallons. An acre-foot is also a measure of volume and is equal to about 325,851 gallons. Hoover Dam near Las Vegas holds 28,500,000 acre-feet of water!

*Dams are constructed from a variety of materials. Arch and gravity dams are built from masonry, while embankment dams are filled with rock, earth, and asphalt. Dams also serve many purposes. Some supply people with water to drink, serve as irrigation for crops, protect areas from flooding, or divert water to a new area.*

*Reservoirs and lakes formed by dams are called impounded lakes and are often used for recreation. Impounded water can be used to generate hydroelectricity. Hydroelectricity is one of the cleanest and cheapest ways to generate energy. Water is held back by the dam to create a reservoir. The weight of the deep water causes pressure against the dam, flowing through the intake with enough force to drive a turbine. The turbine converts flowing water into mechanical energy, which turns into electricity. High-voltage power lines then carry electricity to our homes and businesses.*

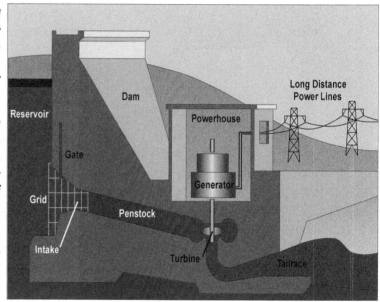

*Bull Shoals Dam is the highest dam in Arkansas at 256 feet above the riverbed—taller than a twenty-story building. Built in 1951, it impounds the White River to form Bull Shoals Lake, one of the largest man-made lakes in the region. 2,100,000 cubic yards of concrete were used to construct this hydroelectric dam. The dam's reservoir is 87 miles in length and has the capacity to store 5,760,000 acre-feet.*

*This map shows the thousands of lakes, reservoirs, rivers, and streams that cover Arkansas, covering over 600,000 acres of land or 1.7% of the state.*

Hunting is the work and sport that involves finding, pursuing, capturing, and/or killing wild animals, usually for food and/or pelts. Fishing involves the catching, taking, or harvesting of fish whether kept or released. Arkansas is noted for its variety of fish and wildlife found across millions of acres. Arkansas's white-tailed deer population is estimated at one million, while bears, geese, elk, and wildfowl are also prevalent. Hunting seasons are set for archery, crossbow, muzzleloaders, and modern guns, but there are no regulated fishing periods. Arkansas is also noted for duck hunting along the famous Mississippi Flyway in the Arkansas Delta and in the Grand Prairie. The Arkansas Game and Fish Commission divides the state into zones to set limits and other regulations.

### *Some of Arkansas's most popular game animals:*

**White-tailed Deer**
(*Odicoileus virginianus*)

**White-tailed Deer (*Odicoileus virginianus*)** was chosen as the official mammal of the state of Arkansas in 1993. In 1916, the state Game and Fish Commission created the first deer season and, as of 2008, the white-tailed deer population sits at roughly one million; the national population is estimated at about 15 million deer. Each year more than 300,000 hunters kill 100,000 deer in Arkansas. In 1999, the Arkansas Game and Fish Commission estimated that 6,000 jobs in our state were directly dependant on the sport of hunting, with annual spending at $300–350 million.

**Eastern Elk (*Cervus canadensis*)** was native to Arkansas but became extinct by the 1840s. Elk populations across North America once numbered in the millions but over-hunting and habitat disruption have reduced the populations. **The Rocky Mountain Elk (*Cervus nelsoni*)** was then introduced in 1933. This herd increased to 200 by the 1950s and then vanished due to illegal hunting and a shrinking habitat. From 1981 to 1985, elk from Colorado and Nebraska were released in Newton County along the Buffalo National River. The herd is now estimated at about 450 animals, and elk hunting was re-established in 1998 with randomly selected permits.

**Eastern Elk**
(*Cervus canadensis*)

### *ELK ZONES (2008)*

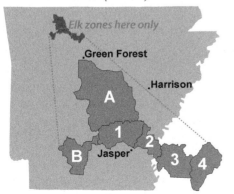

### *BEAR ZONES (2009)*

### *DEER ZONES (2010)*

**Alligators** in Arkansas are protected as a threatened species, but populations are growing due to restoration programs. From 1972 to 1984, more than 2,800 young Louisiana alligators were relocated in southern Arkansas; the current gator population is stable. Alligators represent an excellent example of our ability to revive an endangered species. In Arkansas, we see decreased habitats, but increasing populations indicate effective wildlife management in our state.

**American Alligator**
*(Alligator mississippiensis)*

**DYK?**

Stuttgart, Arkansas, is the "Duck Hunting Capital of the World" and hosts the International Duck Calling Contest and Wings Over the Prairie Festival every Thanksgiving week-end! The first contest and festival were held on November 24, 1936.

Bird or wildfowl hunting begins in the autumn with dove hunting (turtle, mourning), with more than 500,000 killed annually. **Doves (*Streptopelia sp., Zenaida sp.*)** readily adapted to suburban and urban areas and prospered. However, as cities grew, **quails (*Cotumix sp.*)** declined and have halved in number since 1980 due to the destruction of their native habitats, and to an increase in predators (e.g., coyotes). **Wild turkeys (*Meleagris gallopavo*)** and **ducks (*Anas sp.*)** have also increased in numbers since the 1950s due in part to restocking, habitat restoration, and regulated hunting.

**American Mallard**
*(Anas platyrhynchos)*

**Black bears (*Ursus americanus*)** have a long history in our state, once lending Arkansas the nick-name the Bear State. Used for pelts, meat, and fat, bears have been a strong commodity since the colonial period. However, by 1927, due to over-hunting and habitat loss, bears were driven to near extinction, with only 45 bears recorded in Arkansas. Since then, the population has been restored through conservation efforts, hunting restrictions (until the 1980s), and the reintroduction of black bears from Minnesota and Canada. In the 21st century, the Arkansas bear population exceeds 3,000. "Bagged" bears weighing 400–600 pounds are not uncommon in Arkansas.

**Black Bear**
*(Ursus americanus)*

## CANADA GOOSE ZONES

Goose zones here only

## TURKEY ZONES (2010)

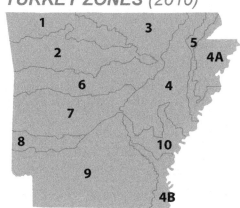

## ALLIGATOR ZONES (2010)

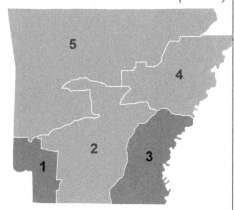

Fishing in Arkansas is a popular sport enjoyed by many. Rainbow, brown, cutthroat, and brook trout are often fished along the White River in the tail waters of the Beaver, Bull Shoals, Greers Ferry, Norfork, and Ouachita dams since trout thrive in cold waters. Mammoth Spring also provides cold water for trout fly-fishing on the Spring River throughout the year. Also, the Little Missouri River in western Arkansas offers cool-season rainbow trout fishing. Catfish, crappie, and bream are also abundant in the southern (Timberlands or lower Delta) part of the state. Bass are fished in streams and lakes in all 75 Arkansas counties. Arkansas has nine species of bass, including stripers that top 60 pounds! Our state currently boasts world records for brown trout, walleye, and hybrid bass.

## COMMON FISH in ARKANSAS

**BASS:** *found in most Arkansas waters with species including striped, shadow, largemouth, rock, smallmouth (or bronzeback), spotted (or Kentucky), and yellowmouth. Larger striped bass can exceed 30–40 pounds (largest: 64lb 8oz in 2000, Beaver Lake tailwaters).*

**BLUEGILL:** *believed to be found in all bodies of water in the state. These fish like cool and warm waters and are rarely caught weighing more than one pound, although a bluegill weighing more than three pounds has been caught (largest: 3l 4oz in 1998, Fulton County Pond).*

**BREAM:** *zoologically these fish are a hybrid between bluegills and sunfish and often display the physical features of both.*

**CARP:** *found in many Arkansas waters with species including bighead, common, black, and silver, with weights often exceeding 50 pounds (largest: 103lb 8oz in 2007, Arkansas River).*

**CATFISH:** *species including blue, channel, and flathead. Have been caught in Arkansas weighing more than 50 pounds (largest: 116lb 12oz in 2001, Mississippi River at West Memphis).*

Fishing involves the catching, taking, or harvesting of fish whether kept or released. Arkansas is noted for its variety of fish and wildlife found across millions of acres. Anglers in Arkansas can find more than 600,000 acres of lakes and more than 9,000 miles of flowing streams and rivers where they can fish for the many species of freshwater fish.

*CRAPPIE: black and white species, rarely larger than four pounds for both (largest: 4lb 9oz in 1976, Oladale Lake).*

*GAR: longnose, shortnose, alligator, and spotted (largest: 35lb 12oz in 2005, Taylor Old River Lake).*

*SUNFISH: green, orange, and spotted species, largest nearly three pounds (largest: 2lb 14oz in 1985, Bois d'Arc Lake).*

*TROUT: found in Arkansas's colder waters with species including brook, brown, rainbow, cutthroat, and lake (largest: 40lb 4oz in 1992, Little Red River—world record).*

*WALLEYE: largest of the perch family, known for its slender body and spiked dorsal fin (largest: 22lb 11oz in 1982, Greers Ferry Lake—world record).*

## FISHERIES Districts

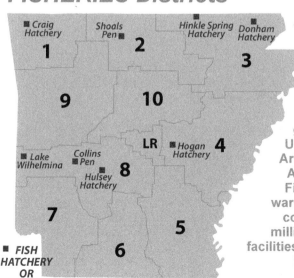

Craig Hatchery — 1
Shoals Pen — 2
Hinkle Spring Hatchery — Donham Hatchery — 3
9
10
Lake Wilhelmina
Collins Pen
LR — Hogan Hatchery — 4
8
Hulsey Hatchery
7
5
6

■ FISH HATCHERY OR CULTURE FACILITY

Arkansas fish hatcheries produce fish species and quantities to establish, maintain, and/or enhance existing fish populations in lakes, rivers, and streams. Most state Game and Fish Commission hatcheries were built between 1928 and 1940 for spawning and raising game fish to stock lakes built by the U.S. Army Corps of Engineers and the Arkansas Game and Fish Commission. As of 2010, the Arkansas Game and Fish Commission operates four warmwater fish hatcheries and one coldwater hatchery, producing millions of fish each year. Culture facilities with net pens are also operated in some bodies of water.

STATE FISH HATCHERY
(WORLD'S LARGEST)
ENTRANCE →
VISITORS WELCOME
Arkansas Game & Fish Commission

The Joe Hogan Fish Hatchery in Lonoke (built in 1928) is the largest state-owned, warm-water fishery in the U.S.

Natural disasters are hazardous events such as volcanic eruptions, floods, tornadoes, tsunamis, or earthquakes that affect communities or human activity. The losses from these natural phenomena depend on the ability of a population to resist or anticipate the disaster, and its ability to recover and mitigate the effects. Many natural hazards can be related, in that an earthquake can trigger a tsunami, or rainfall and flooding can lead to landslides or rockfalls. Arkansas has many hazards, and some disasters have changed history across our state.

## *NEW MADRID EARTHQUAKES of 1811–12*

*In December of 1811, the largest earthquake ever recorded in American history started. This earthquake, which was named for the largest settlement in the area to be devastated—New Madrid, Missouri—revealed an active fault line extending through several states. From the effects of the 1811–12 earthquakes, it can be estimated that they had a magnitude of 8.0 or higher on the not-yet-invented Richter scale. Large areas sank into the earth, new lakes formed, and the Mississippi River changed its course due to the intense shaking. Here is a map of the Mercalli intensity values that have been estimated by looking at the destruction of structures nearly two hundred years ago. Such an earthquake now could kill thousands of people and animals and cost Arkansas billions of dollars in damages, as well as enormous human costs.*

**DYK?**

**WHAT IS THE MERCALLI SCALE?**

I. Not felt by many people.
II. Felt only by a few people at best.
III. Felt quite noticeably by people indoors.
IV. Felt indoors; dishes, windows, doors disturbed.
V. Felt outside by most; dishes and windows break; bells ring.
VI. Felt by all; glassware breaks and books fall off shelves; heavy furniture moves.
VII. Difficult to stand; furniture breaks; damage in poorly built structures.
VIII. Damage in poorly built structures; chimneys fall; heavy furniture moves.
IX. General panic; buildings shift off foundations.
X. Most buildings destroyed.
XI. Bridges and buildings completely destroyed.
XII. Damage is total!

**Mercalli ratings for the New Madrid Earthquakes**

There are many ways to measure the strength of an earthquake, but the most common methods are the Mercalli and Richter scales.

*The Mercalli scale was invented in 1902 and uses observations of the event or its effects on structures to estimate the earthquake's intensity from a range of I (not noticeable) to XII (complete devastation). Mercalli is widely used but since it relies on the subjectivity of human observations, it is often less accurate than scientific scales like Richter. Invented by Charles Richter in 1935, the Richter scale is calculated from the amplitude of the largest seismic wave recorded for the earthquake and ranges from 1 to 10.*

*" I was roused from sleep by the clamor of windows, doors and furniture in tremulous motion, with a distant rumbling noise, resembling a number of carriages passing over pavement—in a few seconds the motion and subterraneous thunder increased more and more. The agitation had now reached its utmost violence. The sky was obscured by a thick hazy fog, without a breath of air.  Later another shock occurred nearly as tremulous as the first, but without as much noise, it lasted about fifty seconds, and a slight trembling continued at intervals for some time after."*

**Saturday, December 21, 1811 (*Louisiana Gazette*, St. Louis)**

# Disasters

## GREAT FLOOD of 1927

The Flood of 1927 was the most destructive and costly disaster in American history, with 6,600 square miles flooded and 36 of 75 Arkansas counties under water. About 350,000 people and 2,000,000 acres of farmland were affected, and 40,000 families received relief. One hundred people died in Arkansas with losses in Arkansas totaling over $1 million in 1927 dollars. The Mississippi River remained at flood stage for 153 days. Warm weather and early snow melts caused the Mississippi River to rise, so with heavy rainfall in April, the already full rivers swelled. Parts of Arkansas were also severely flooded in 1937.

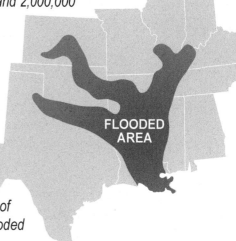

FLOODED AREA

## TORNADOES

Tornadoes are rotating columns of air that often make destructive contact with the Earth's surface. They typically occur when swirling air descends from cumulonimbus or cumulus clouds. Many tornadoes have wind speeds between 40 and 120 mph (64–180 kph). In rare cases, they have been measured with wind speeds of more than 300 mph (500 kph). Although tornadoes have been observed everywhere except Antarctica, most occur in the U.S. Tornado Alley. In some cases, these strong winds can lift and heave heavy objects like railroad cars many feet.

April 3-4, 2008, twister damage at Little Rock Airport

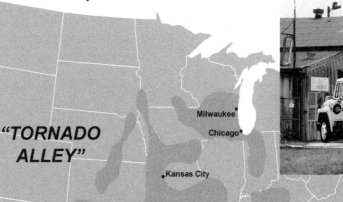

"TORNADO ALLEY"

Milwaukee
Chicago
Kansas City
Tulsa
Oklahoma City
Amarillo
Little Rock
Birmingham
Atlanta
Fort Worth
Dallas
Jackson
Baton Rouge
Houston
Orlando

**TORNADOES**

6 to 10

11 to 15

> 15

*average per year per 1,000 square miles*

Compared with other states, Arkansas ranks 16th in tornado occurrence and 4th in number of related fatalities, but 17th in the overall damages. If we look at Arkansas's statistics from 1950 to 1995, more than 3,500 tornadoes have cost Arkansas more than 500 million dollars!

# GLOSSARY

AGRICULTURE: production of food, goods, or services in livestock, farming, or forestry. Rice is Arkansas's top agricultural crop.

ARCHAIC ERA: period when native peoples thrived through sedentary lifestyles ca. 9500 BC to ca. 650 BC. (see WOODLAND ERA)

CARTOGRAPHY: science and art of making maps, including history, technology, psychology, and visualization of maps.

CIVIL WAR: occurred 1861–1865 when eleven southern states seceded from the U.S. and formed the Confederacy led by Jefferson Davis. Significant battles followed until the Union won.

CLIMATOLOGY: study of Earth's atmosphere, temperature, humidity, air pressure, and precipitation over the current long term and in the past. (see METEOROLOGY)

DAM: natural or constructed barrier that impounds water, often made for water collection, irrigation, flood protection, and/or recreation.

DEMOGRAPHY: study of the characteristics of a population, including race, ethnicity, gender, income, education attained, disabilities, location, and employment. A census is used to collect these data for study.

DESOTO EXPEDITION: first group of European explorers to visit Arkansas, in 1541.

DIAMOND: mineral composed of pure carbon, found only in Arkansas in the U.S. It is one of the most valuable materials found on Earth.

DISTORTION: stretching and compression on a map when a flat map is created to show the curving, spherical surface of a planet.

EARTH: third planet from the sun, and the fifth-largest in our solar system. It is also called Terra, Blue Planet, or our world.

ECOSYSTEM: environmental systems that include the combined components of the botanical (plants), zoological (animals), and physical (climate, geology). (see ENVIRON-MENT, ENDANGERED SPECIES)

ELEVATION: height above sea level measured in feet, me-ters, miles, or kilometers. Variation in elevation is called relief.

ENDANGERED SPECIES: plant or animal species on the brink of extinction, often as a function of a destroyed or failing habitat.

ENVIRONMENT: natural landscape that encompasses all living (biotic) and non-living (abiotic) things occurring naturally on Earth.

ENVIRONMENTAL LAPSE RATE: change in temperature as a function of elevation—air cools as we ascend, air warms as we descend. In dry conditions it is 5.5°F for every 1,000' (10°C/1,000m) and in wet conditions it is 3.6°F for every 1,000' (6.5°C/1,000m).

ETHNICITY: the grouping of humans based on similarities including distinctive culture, religion, language, and regional traits.

FISHING: catching, taking, and/or harvesting of fish whether kept or released. In Arkansas, game fish include bass, bluegill, bream, carp, catfish, crappie, gar, sunfish, trout, and walleye.

FIVE CIVILIZED TRIBES: five Native American nations of Cherokee, Chickasaw, Choctaw, Creek, and Seminole who were relocated between 1830 and 1839. (see TRAIL OF TEARS)

GEOGRAPHY: study of all aspects of our landscape, including economic, physical, cultural, and political landscapes. (see MILIEU)

GEOLOGY: study of the structure, composition, and history of Earth's physical material and the processes by which it is formed.

HAZARD: natural or human-induced disaster, including tornadoes, floods, volcanoes, earthquakes, hurricanes, and landslides.

HUNTING: sport and work involving finding, pursuing, capturing, and/or killing animals for food, pelts, or sport. Arkansas's hunted game includes bears, Canada geese, deer, elk, and turkeys.

INDUSTRY: manufacturing of goods or services; includes five sectors (1st raw materials, 2nd manufacturing/construction, 3rd consumer services, 4th business services, 5th information services).

KARST: landscapes formed from the dissolving of soluble rocks like limestone, resulting in extensive underground cave, river, and tunnel systems. Northwest Arkansas is a karst region. (see SPELEOTHEM)

LAMPROITE: rock material in which diamonds are formed and found in Arkansas at the Crater of Diamonds State Park. Related to kimberlite, the most common diamond-bearing rock on Earth.

LATITUDE: Earth's imaginary lines that are parallel to the equator and range from 0°–90° north and south. The equator is latitude 0°, and the North and South poles are points at 90°.

LEGEND: map key that explains representative symbols on the map that represent features on the landscape. (see CARTOGRAPHY)

LOCATION: absolute or relative position in physical space that something occupies on a surface. (see LATITUDE, LONGITUDE)

LONGITUDE: Earth's imaginary lines that run from pole to pole and range from 0°–180° east and west. All lines of longitude are equal in length and begin at the Prime Meridian (0°) that runs through Greenwich, England (near London). (see LATITUDE)

LOUISIANA PURCHASE: extensive land purchase in 1803 from France by the United States, amounting to 828,800 square miles of land or parts of 14 U.S. states and two Canadian provinces. It cost 60 million francs and the cancellation of an 18 million franc debt (a total of $15 million in 1803).

MAP: representation of the real landscape rendered on paper or computer, usually smaller than the actual space. These include reference maps and thematic maps. (see CARTOGRAPHY, LEGEND)

METEOROLOGY: study of Earth's short-term weather and weather patterns. Long-term study of weather is called climatology.

MILIEU: all objects, actions, and processes represented on Earth's surface; all surroundings on our landscape. (see GEOGRAPHY)

MINERAL: naturally occurring material formed through geologic processes that have distinctive chemical, physical, and optical properties, like diamond or quartz. (see ROCK)

MINING: process of removing useful and/or valuable rocks, minerals, or other materials from veins, seams, and ore bodies or from massive deposits in the earth. (see GEOLOGY, MINERAL, ROCK)

MISSISSIPPI ERA: ca. AD 900–1600, a time of community development with temple mounds and increased agricultural development.

PALEO-INDIAN ERA: era of the arrival of the earliest Native Americans to Arkansas approximately 13,500 years ago.

PHOTOGRAMMETRY: science of using aerial photography and other remote-sensing images to obtain measurement of geological features.

POLITICS: activities and processes involved in guiding a political entity like a city, county, state, or country.

POPULATION DENSITY: a measure of population that examines people per area. (see DEMOGRAPHY)

PROJECTION: technique used in cartography to convert a curved surface on Earth to a flat map. (see CARTOGRAPHY, DISTORTION)

PROTECTED LANDS: land set aside for the conservation of natural ecosystems, including national and state parks, refuges, and wilderness areas. (see ENVIRONMENT, ECOSYSTEM, ENDANGERED)

RACE: categorization of humans based on inherited and observed characteristics, including skin color, facial features, and hair texture.

REGION: area of similar characteristics that might include language, culture, physical features, government, religion, and/or landforms.

REMOTE SENSING: art and science of obtaining information about Earth's features from measurements using satellites and aircraft.

ROCK: combination or aggregate of one or more minerals. For example, granite is a rock composed of minerals like quartz, feldspar, and mica. (see GEOLOGY, MINERAL, MINING)

SCALE: relationship between the actual size of land or water on Earth and its size represented on a map. Often represented as a fraction or bar. (see CARTOGRAPHY, PROJECTION, DISTORTION)

SPELEOTHEM: cave formation formed by the deposition of minerals, like calcium carbonate. These fragile shapes include stalactites, stalagmites, columns, flowstone, and crystals. (see KARST)

TRAIL OF TEARS: forced relocation of 46,000 Native Americans from their homelands to Indian Territory (present-day Oklahoma) in 1830–1839. Many died en route, while others suffered from starvation, disease, and exposure. (see FIVE CIVILIZED TRIBES)

WOODLAND ERA: period of expansion for native peoples through hunting, gathering, and agriculture, ca. 600 BC to AD 1000. (see ARCHAIC ERA)

# UNIQUE Arkansas!

**OFFICIAL STATE THINGS ...**

State Mammal: White-tailed deer
State Beverage: Milk
State Bird: Mockingbird
State Butterfly: Diana fritillary
State Dance: Square dance
State Fish: Largemouth bass
State Flower: Apple blossom
State Gemstone: Diamond
State Insect: Honeybee
State Instrument: Fiddle
State Mineral: Quartz
State Motto: Regnat Populus
State Rock: Bauxite
State Soil: Stuttgart Series
State Tree: Pine

## DYK?

### some FAMOUS ARKANSANS

Bill Clinton, 42nd President
Douglas MacArthur, Army General
J. William Fulbright, Politician
Sam Walton, Wal-Mart Founder
Maya Angelou, Author-Poet
Johnny Cash, Singer-Songwriter
Jermain Taylor, Boxing Champ
Scott Joplin, Composer
E. Fay Jones, Architect
Eldridge Cleaver, Author-Activist
Glen Campbell, Musician

**Alma:** Spinach Capital of the World
**Cotter:** Trout Capital of the U.S.A.
**Emerson:** World Championship Rotary Tiller Race
**Eureka Springs:** America's largest free-standing rock, Pivot Rock
**Heber Springs:** World Championship Cardboard Boat Races
**Hope:** Watermelon Capital of the World and birthplace of Bill Clinton
**Hot Springs:** First national park (Reservation) (1832, made official in 1921)
**Hot Springs:** World's shortest street, Bridge Street at 98 feet
**Hot Springs Village:** America's largest gated community (26,000 acres)
**Little Rock:** Largest collection in any presidential library, Clinton Library
**Magnolia:** World Championship Steak Cook-off
**Magnolia:** World's largest charcoal grill (70')
**Malvern:** Brick Capital of the World
**Mount Ida:** Quartz Crystal Capital of the World
**Mountain View:** Great Arkansas Outhouse Race
**Mountain View:** Folk Music Capital of the World
**Murfreesboro:** America's only diamond mine
**Pine Bluff:** Archery Bow Capital of the World
**Stuttgart:** Rice Capital of the World; Duck Hunting Capital of the World
**Stuttgart:** World's Championship Duck-Calling Contest

# GAZETTEER

*city name (population 2010 census)*       *map location*

|  |  |
|---|---|
| Arkadelphia (10,714) | C-7 |
| Bald Knob NWR | P-4 |
| Batesville (10,248) | F-2 |
| Beaver Lake | L-1 |
| Bella Vista (26,461) | A-1 |
| Benton (30,681) | D-5 |
| Big Lake NWR | S-2 |
| Buffalo Natl. River Wilderness | M,N,O-2 |
| Bentonville (35,301) | A-1 |
| Blytheville (15,620) | J-2 |
| Bryant (16,688) | E-5 |
| Cache River NWR | Q-3,4,5 |
| Caney Creek Wilderness | K-6 |
| Cabot (23,776) | E-4 |
| Camden (12,183) | D-8 |
| Clarksville (9,178) | C-3 |
| Conway (58,908) | E-4 |
| Crossett (5,507) | E-9 |
| De Queen (6,594) | A-7 |
| Dry Creek Wilderness | L-4 |
| East Fork Wilderness | N-3 |
| El Dorado (18,884) | D-9 |
| Fayetteville (73,580) | A-2 |
| Felsenthal NWR | O-9 |
| Flatside Wilderness | M,N-5 |
| Forrest City (15,371) | H-4 |
| Fort Smith (86,209) | A-3,4 |
| Greenwood (8,952) | A-4 |
| Harrison (12,943) | C-1 |
| Heber Springs (7,165) | E-3 |
| Helena-West Helena (12,282) | H-6 |
| Holla Bend NWR | M,N-4 |
| Hope (10,095) | B-8 |
| Hot Springs (35,193) | C-6 |
| Hot Springs Natl. Park | M-6 |
| Hot Springs Village (12,807) | D-5 |
| Hurricane Creek Wilderness | M-3 |
| Jacksonville (28,364) | E-5 |
| Jonesboro (67,263) | H-2 |
| Leatherwood Wilderness | O-2 |
| Little Rock/North Little Rock (255,828) | E-5 |
| Lowell (7,327) | A-1 |
| Magnolia (11,577) | C-9 |
| Malvern (10,318) | D-6 |
| Marion (12,345) | J-4 |
| Maumelle (17,163) | E-5 |
| Memphis, TN (646,889) | J-4 |
| Mena (5,737) | A-5 |
| Monticello (9,467) | F-8 |
| Morrilton (6,767) | D-4 |
| Mountain Home (12,448) | E-1 |
| Newport (7,879) | G-3 |
| Osceola (7,757) | J-3 |
| Ouachita NF | K,L,M,N-4, 5; K,L,M-6 |
| Overflow NWR | P-9 |
| Ozark NF | K,L,M,N-2,3; O-2; L,M-4 |
| Paragould (26,113) | H-2 |
| Pea Ridge Natl. Military Park | L-1 |
| Pine Bluff (49,083) | E-6 |
| Pocahontas (6,608) | G-1 |
| Pond Creek NWR | K-7 |
| Poteau Mountain Wilderness | K-4 |
| Richland Creek Wilderness | N-2 |
| Rogers (55,964) | B-1 |
| Russellville (27,920) | C-4 |
| Saint Francis NF | R-5 |
| Searcy (22,858) | F-4 |
| Sherwood (29,523) | E-5 |
| Siloam Springs (15,039) | A-2 |
| Springdale (69,797) | B-1,2 |
| Stuttgart (9,326) | F-6 |
| Texarkana (29,919) | B-8 |
| Trumann (7,243) | H-3 |
| Upper Buffalo Wilderness | M-2 |
| Van Buren (22,791) | A-3 |
| Wapanocca NWR | S-4 |
| Warren (6,003) | E-8 |
| West Memphis (26,245) | J-4 |
| White River NWR | Q-6 |
| Wynne (8,367) | H-4 |

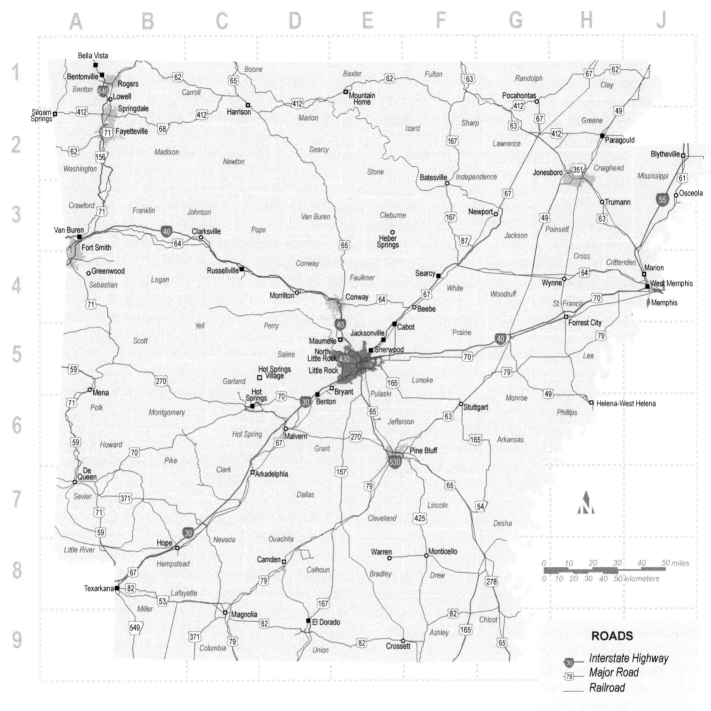

**ROADS**

 **30** Interstate Highway

**79** Major Road

Railroad

**CITY POPULATION (2010)**

○ 5,001 - 10,000*

□ 10,001 - 20,000

■ 20,001 - 40,000

40,001 - 90,000

> 90,000

*Towns with populations <5,000 are too numerous to show

Bella Vista
Bentonville
Rogers
Lowell
Springdale
Siloam Springs
Fayetteville
Harrison
Mountain Home
Pocahontas
Paragould
Blytheville
Osceola
Van Buren
Fort Smith
Clarksville
Batesville
Jonesboro
Trumann
Greenwood
Russellville
Newport
Marion
West Memphis
Heber Springs
Searcy
Wynne
Morrilton
Conway
Beebe
Memphis
Maumelle
Jacksonville
Cabot
Forrest City
North Little Rock
Sherwood
Little Rock
Mena
Hot Springs Village
Bryant
Stuttgart
Helena-West Helena
Hot Springs
Benton
Pine Bluff
Malvern
De Queen
Arkadelphia
Warren
Monticello
Hope
Camden
Texarkana
Magnolia
El Dorado
Crossett

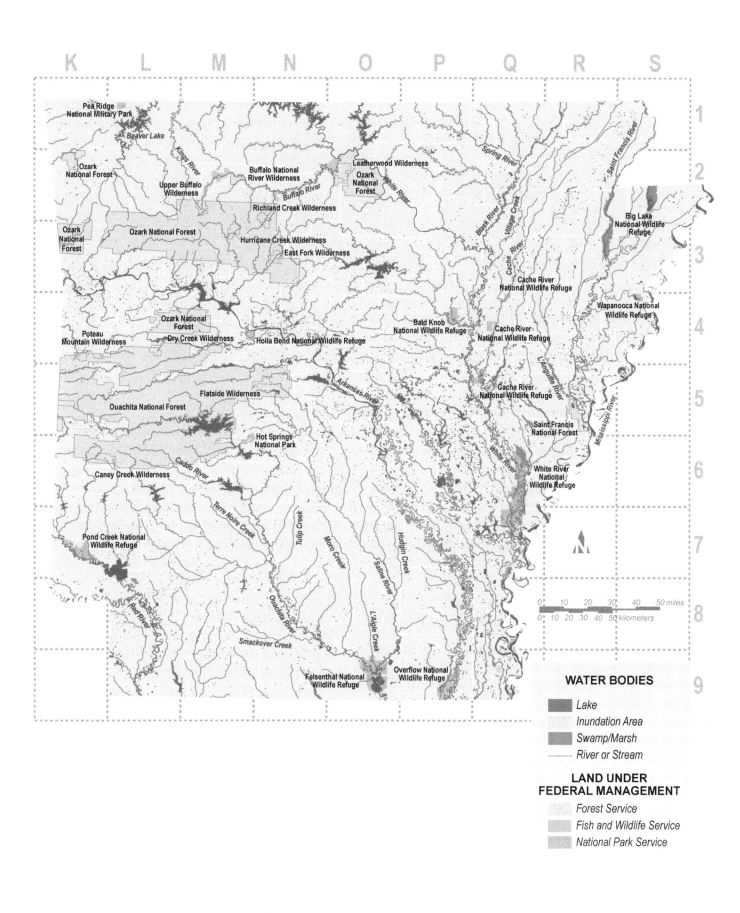

K L M N O P Q R S

1
2
3
4
5
6
7
8
9

Pea Ridge
National Military Park

Beaver Lake

Kings River

Ozark
National Forest

Upper Buffalo
Wilderness

Buffalo National
River Wilderness

Leatherwood Wilderness

Ozark
National
Forest

White River

Spring River

Saint Francis River

Ozark
National
Forest

Ozark National Forest

Richland Creek Wilderness

Hurricane Creek Wilderness

East Fork Wilderness

Buffalo River

Black River

Village Creek

Big Lake
National Wildlife
Refuge

Cache River

Cache River
National Wildlife
Refuge

Poteau
Mountain Wilderness

Ozark National
Forest

Dry Creek Wilderness

Holla Bend National Wildlife Refuge

Bald Knob
National Wildlife Refuge

Cache River
National
Wildlife Refuge

Wapanocca National
Wildlife Refuge

Flatside Wilderness

Ouachita National Forest

Hot Springs
National Park

Arkansas River

L'Anguille River

Cache River
National Wildlife
Refuge

Saint Francis
National Forest

Mississippi River

Caney Creek Wilderness

Caddo River

White River

White River
National
Wildlife Refuge

Pond Creek National
Wildlife Refuge

Terre Noire Creek

Tulip Creek

Moro Creek

Saline River

Hudgin Creek

Red River

Ouachita River

Smackover Creek

L'Aigle Creek

Felsenthal National
Wildlife Refuge

Overflow National
Wildlife Refuge

0 10 20 30 40 50 miles
0 10 20 30 40 50 kilometers

## WATER BODIES

Lake
Inundation Area
Swamp/Marsh
River or Stream

## LAND UNDER
## FEDERAL MANAGEMENT

Forest Service
Fish and Wildlife Service
National Park Service

**Encyclopedia of Arkansas History & Culture.** *www.encyclopediaofarkansas.net*
The Encyclopedia of Arkansas, a project of the Butler Center for Arkansas Studies at the Central Arkansas Library System, is the premier one-stop reference on all aspects of the state's history and culture, promoting the study, understanding, and appreciation of Arkansas's heritage. The online encyclopedia is continually updated to provide a comprehensive look at Arkansas for historians, teachers, students, and anyone interested in the Natural State.

**Butler Center for Arkansas Studies.** *www.butlercenter.org*
The Butler Center for Arkansas Studies promotes understanding and appreciation of Arkansas history, literature, art, and culture. In addition to providing public access to manuscripts, books, maps, photographs, and databases in the Research Room at the Arkansas Studies Institute building in Little Rock, the Butler Center offers a book-publishing program, an oral history project, workshops and other training programs, public lectures and events, and support for teachers of Arkansas history.

**Department of Arkansas Heritage.** *www.arkansasheritage.com*
The Department of Arkansas Heritage preserves and promotes Arkansas's proud natural and cultural heritage, overseeing projects including the Delta Cultural Center, the Historic Arkansas Museum, the Old State House Museum, and the Mosaic Templars Cultural Center.

**Arkansas History Commission.** *www.ark-ives.com*
The Arkansas History Commission and State Archives, located in Little Rock, is the official state archives of Arkansas and houses the state's largest collection of documents, publications, photographs, and other material relating to Arkansas history.

**Special Collections, University of Arkansas.** *http://libinfo.uark.edu/SpecialCollections*
The UA Special Collections Department encourages research and writing in the history and culture of Arkansas and the surrounding region. The department provides public access to historical manuscripts, archives, maps, photographs, and published materials to support scholarly investigation of the state, its customs and people, and its cultural, physical, and political climate.

**Arkansas Department of Parks and Tourism.** *www.arkansas.com*
The Arkansas Department of Parks and Tourism manages the state's fifty-two state parks and promotes the state of Arkansas as a tourist destination.

**Arkansas Geological Survey.** *www.geology.ar.gov*
An agency of the Arkansas state government, the Arkansas Geological Survey investigates the geology, geological processes, and geological resources of the state, encouraging the effective management of resources and consideration for the environment. The AGS presents community outreach talks and field trips to schools, organizations, and other groups.

**Arkansas Game and Fish Commission.** *http://www.agfc.com*
The Arkansas Game and Fish Commission oversees the protection, conservation, and preservation of fish and wildlife in Arkansas through habitat management, fish stocking, hunting and fishing regulations, and many other programs. The AGFC also provides many programs for the public to generate awareness of sound environmental management to ensure a healthy wildlife population for future generations.

CPSIA information can be obtained
at www.ICGtesting.com
Printed in the USA
FSOW04n0215030317
31339FS